THE NOUVELLE CUISINE OF JEAN & PIERRE TROISGROS

THE NOUVELLE CUISINE OF JEAN & PIERRE TROISGROS

BY JEAN&PIERRE TROISGROS

Translated by Roberta Wolfe Smoler

WILLIAM MORROW AND COMPANY, INC.
New York

BOOK DESIGN BY SALLIE BALDWIN, ANTLER & BALDWIN, INC.

Color photography by Didier Blanchat

Translation copyright © 1978 by William Morrow & Company, Inc.

Originally published in French under the title *Cuisiniers à Roanne*, copyright © 1977 by Editions Robert Laffont, S.A.

Library of Congress Cataloging in Publication Data

Troisgros, Jean (date)
    The nouvelle cuisine of Jean & Pierre Troisgros.

    Translation of Cuisiniers à Roanne.
    Includes index.
    1. Cookery, French. 2. Roanne, France—
Social life and customs. I. Troisgros, Pierre,
(date) joint author. II. Title.
TX719.T7613   641.5'944'52   78-19174
ISBN 0-688-03331-8

Printed in the United States of America.

First Edition

1 2 3 4 5 6 7 8 9 10

Preface

France, decade after decade, has produced untold numbers of talented chefs. And yet, even in France, in a generation only a few creative geniuses emerge who can be said to have altered the course of great cuisine.

During the 1950s, as the great restaurants flourished again after World War II, young apprentices once more trained arduously to learn the classic disciplines. An unusual number of them were lucky enough to have had both creative talent and creative mentors. Among them were Jean and Pierre Troisgros, who worked in the kitchen of Fernand Point, one of the great innovators of an earlier generation.

Before the decade was out, a coterie of new young chefs, young Turks, if you will, appeared at the helm of their own restaurants with classic training but with a new central idea—that great cooking for modern times should be innovative and creative, not hidebound by classic rules, and that it should be lighter, more respectful of ingredients, and thereby more delicious and more honest than before.

From this way of thinking among the new chefs came the now famous term *nouvelle cuisine*—the new French cooking. It is not well understood, especially outside of France, that *nouvelle cuisine* is a creative point of view toward cooking, not a codified repertory to which a *nouvelle* label is to be applied. Codification is exactly what the new chefs abhor, and if the menus in their restaurants sometimes list similar dishes, this is for the reason, also new, that they exchange information about their experiments, sharing ideas in a pioneer spirit.

The Nouvelle Cuisine of Jean & Pierre Troisgros

Jean Troisgros was born in 1926 and Pierre Troisgros in 1928 at Chalon-sur-Saône, where their father, Jean-Baptiste, owned a local café. Jean-Baptiste Troisgros was a Burgundian who loved the cooking and the wines of his province. He would have liked to have been a chef, and from their earliest years he influenced his sons to make their careers as chefs.

In 1930, the Troisgros family moved to the Hôtel des Platanes (which today houses the Troisgros restaurant) on the Place de la Gare at Roanne in the Lyonnais. The restaurant at that time was a modest one frequented by traveling salesmen who gathered around a central table to enjoy the congenial atmosphere, the fine wines of Monsieur Troisgros, and the excellent home cooking of Madame Troisgros.

The Troisgros brothers received their classic training at the restaurant Lucas-Carton in Paris, where the young Paul Bocuse also trained with them. They then went to Vienne to work at La Pyramide for Fernand Point and returned to Roanne in 1953. Established in their own kitchen, they earned their first star in the *Guide Michelin* in 1955, their second in 1965, and their third in 1968. In the next decade their fame grew the world over as chefs and as chefs of the *nouvelle cuisine*.

Jean Troisgros has one son and Pierre Troisgros two; all three are chefs.

THE PUBLISHERS

6

Contents

The Nouvelle Cuisine of Jean & Pierre Troisgros

Introduction

OUR FATHER, JEAN-BAPTISTE TROISGROS, used to say that "cooking should be a harmony of the treasures of the good earth." He was not a chef (and was consoled in this only by inculcating in us from childhood the vocation he had been denied), but he had an innate sense of true cuisine; we owe to him many of the ideas that seemed to be so revolutionary in the 1950s.

He did not like the all-purpose sauce stocks that were then being used in many of the greatest restaurants and made us eliminate them as well as the binding—*liaison*—of sauces with flour or other starches.

He did not like dishes finished by a *maître d'hôtel* in the dining room; the chef should be responsible for his cooking to the end.

He did not like complicated platters and presentations, and from this came the custom of both presentation and service on each guest's individual plate—very large plates, which we were the first to use.

Nor did he like traditional *garnitures*: the steamed potato, the tomato, the watercress, the sautéed croûtons that uselessly encumber the plate and contribute nothing to the dish.

But he loved fine produce, as we do. We get our fresh snails from the schoolboys of Roanne, who hunt them in the wild nearby. From the native kitchen gardeners we get their best fresh vegetables, and the salmon comes to us from the fishermen on our local river, the Allier. We get our lobsters from Brittany, our chickens from Bresse. And, as good housewives do, we market every morning and buy only the produce in season, the best, of irreproachable quality and freshness.

We respect these treasures of the earth of which our father spoke. Why damage or mask the flavor of fine meat, the verdant freshness of spring vegetables? Precise timing and delicate sauces divested of complication—to accompany, perhaps to exalt, but always to allow ingredients to be what they are—these are what we try to achieve.

In becoming simpler and lighter, the cuisine of the chef has made a *rapprochement* to that of the *ménagère*, the French home cook. This is what we have tried to demonstrate by publishing our personal recipes.

JEAN and PIERRE TROISGROS

Editor's Note

The recipes in this edition of THE NOUVELLE CUISINE OF JEAN & PIERRE TROISGROS have been tested in the translator's American home kitchen. This produced information about the way in which certain recipes work that does not appear in the original French. Information concerning American ingredients and substitutions for unobtainable French ingredients has also been added. All such material not contained in the French text is printed in *italic* type.

THE NOUVELLE CUISINE OF JEAN & PIERRE TROISGROS

Les fonds

BASIC PREPARATIONS

Though the use of stocks is becoming less prevalent than it once was in French cuisine, stocks do continue to be an important part of the making of fine sauces.

We have provided in this chapter recipes for brown stocks and light stocks and for *court-bouillon* for fish and seafood, willingly eliminating the more complicated formulas that are burdensome to make in a home kitchen.

We rarely use flour-based *roux* in sauces anymore and use instead reductions of stocks and cooking liquids and simple *liaisons* made with butter added at the last.

Formerly, it was necessary to make stocks no sooner than the day before using them, or even on the same day. Now, with efficient home freezers being common, stocks may be prepared once or twice a month, or only as often as you need them. Store them in your freezer in small plastic containers, as small as a cup or pint and only a few as large as a quart in capacity. The containers must have very close-fitting lids and it is wise to label them as to their contents and the dates when they were frozen.

Our recipes for stocks in this book are for modest quantities. They are easily multiplied if you wish to make larger supplies for freezing.

Among the best substitutes for a stock made according to these recipes is the bouillon from a poached chicken or from old-fashioned boiled beef (*pot-au-feu*, of which Americans have their own versions).

These bouillons, too, may be saved and stored in your freezer. As a last resort, commercial concentrates and bouillon cubes dissolved in boiling water may be used, but these broths certainly must be "refreshed" by simmering with fresh vegetables, herbs, mushroom peelings when you have them, and crushed peppercorns.

Fond blanc de volaille
CHICKEN STOCK

To make about 3 quarts chicken stock:
    2½ pounds chicken carcasses, necks, wing tips, and (*if possible*)
        feet
    1 carrot, sliced
    1 onion, sliced
    1 leek, white part only
    1 small stalk celery
    2 cloves garlic
    1 clove
    1 teaspoon peppercorns, slightly crushed

PREPARATION:

Place the chicken bones in a large stockpot and add cold water to cover. Bring the water slowly to a boil, and skim the surface carefully to remove all scum.

Add the vegetables and spices, then regulate the heat to maintain a steady boil. Cook 1 hour, removing fat as it rises to the surface. If the stock is skimmed carefully, it will remain clear.

Strain the stock through a fine sieve. There should be about 3 quarts. Cool, and refrigerate or freeze it until ready to use.

Fond de veau brun

BROWN VEAL STOCK

To make about 1 quart veal stock:

  2½ pounds veal knuckle and leg bones, cut into manageable pieces
    (ask your butcher to do this)
  1 large onion, sliced
  2 carrots, sliced
  1 clove garlic
  Bouquet garni (sprigs of thyme and parsley and a bay leaf, tied
    together)

PREPARATION:

Preheat oven to 475° F.

Spread out the bones on a large baking sheet. Roast, turning them once or twice, until well browned on all sides (*allow about 45 minutes; Ed.*).

Place the hot bones in a large stockpot with the onion, carrot, garlic, and *bouquet garni*. Do not add salt. Fill the pot with enough cold water to cover the ingredients and bring to a vigorous boil. Then skim off the surface scum.

Let the stock boil gently for about 4 hours. Frequently skim off the scum and fat that will continue to rise to the surface. Strain through a fine sieve. There should be about 1 quart brown veal stock.

When the broth has cooled, lift off any excess fat with a large shallow spoon. Refrigerate or freeze the stock until ready to use.

Demi-glace tomatée

CONCENTRATED VEAL STOCK WITH TOMATO

To make 1 pint *demi-glace*:

  2 tablespoons peanut oil
  1 small carrot, finely chopped
  1 small onion, finely chopped

3 fresh tomatoes, chopped
½ tablespoon tomato paste
1 stalk celery, cut into several pieces
Parsley sprigs, tied together
1 quart Brown Veal Stock (*fond de veau brun*, page 17)
5 peppercorns, slightly crushed

PREPARATION:

The *demi-glace* is based on a reduction of veal stock and aromatic vegetables.

Heat the oil in a heavy medium-size casserole. Add the *mirepoix* of carrot and onion and cook, covered, over low heat to release their juices. Add the tomatoes and, when the vegetables are soft, stir in the tomato paste. Add the celery, parsley, and stock, and bring to a boil. Then reduce heat to the barest simmer and cook 1 hour. Skim the surface occasionally and add pepper during the final 10 minutes of cooking.

When finished, the stock should be reduced by half, with only 1 pint remaining. Cook longer if necessary.

Strain the *demi-glace* through a fine sieve. Cool, and refrigerate or freeze it until ready to use.

Glace de viande
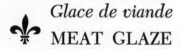
MEAT GLAZE

This is obtained by slowly reducing veal stock until it becomes a dark-brown, syrupy glaze. Meat glaze is used in preparing *steak au poivre* and to enrich sauces.

To make about 1½ cups meat glaze:
    4 quarts (or more) Brown Veal Stock (*fond de veau brun*, page 17)

PREPARATION:

Let the stock reduce over very low heat, and, using a ladle, carefully remove the sediment which forms on the sides of the casserole. The clarity of the glaze depends on this. As the reduction proceeds, transfer the liquid to smaller, more suitable saucepans.

The liquid must reduce by nine-tenths its original volume and the finished glaze must be clear, syrupy, and bright. For these reasons you should begin with at least 4 quarts of stock.

The reduction time is variable, depending upon the degree of heat being used. Though it is impossible to give a precise cooking time, start the reduction early in the day as it will need more than a few hours for completion.

Fond de gibier
GAME STOCK

To make 1 quart game stock:

> 2 pounds carcasses and giblets from feathered game, or trimmings (sinews and fell) from furred game
> 3 tablespoons peanut oil
> 1 carrot, finely chopped
> 1 onion, finely chopped
> *Bouquet garni* (sprigs of thyme and parsley and a bay leaf, tied together)
> 4 cups red wine
> 2 cups Concentrated Veal Stock with Tomato (*demi-glace tomatée,* page 17)

PREPARATION:

Heat the oil in a casserole, and brown the miscellaneous bones and trimmings, turning them frequently. Allow about 10 minutes for this operation.

Add the *mirepoix* of carrot and onion, and continue cooking until they are also lightly browned. Add the *bouquet garni* and moisten with red wine and *demi-glace.* Bring to a boil, then reduce heat to low, and simmer the stock for 3 hours. Skim the surface frequently and, as necessary, add enough water to keep the ingredients covered.

Strain the broth through a fine sieve and skim off all fat. Cool the stock, and refrigerate or freeze it until ready to use.

Fumet de poisson
FISH STOCK

To make about 1 quart fish stock:
- 2 to 2½ pounds heads and bones from any fresh, white-fleshed (non-oily) fish
- 1 onion, thinly sliced
- *Bouquet garni* (sprigs of thyme and parsley and a bay leaf, tied together)

PREPARATION:

Rinse the fish bones well in several changes of cold water, then place them in a large heavy casserole with the onion. Cook 10 minutes, covered, over low heat to release their juices. Turn them frequently. (*Take care with this operation because there is no addition of oil or fat to prevent the bones and onion from sticking to the casserole. Ed.*)

Add cold water to cover and the *bouquet garni*. Bring the liquid slowly to a boil and skim the surface until no trace of scum remains. Then reduce heat to a simmer and cook 25 minutes.

Strain through a fine sieve lined with dampened cheesecloth and, when cool, refrigerate or freeze. Because the stock will jell when chilled, it is preferable to strain it into storage containers before it congeals.

NOTE: If desired, you may replace one-third of the water with 1 cup of dry white wine; however, we prefer to keep the character of the *fumet* neutral, leaving freedom for the future enhancement of a variety of fish and shellfish.

Nage pour poissons, crustacés, ou coquillages
COURT-BOUILLON

To make 3 quarts *court-bouillon*:
- 6 carrots, about 1 pound
- 3 stalks celery
- 3 small onions, sliced, about ½ pound

6 shallots, sliced
1 whole head garlic, unpeeled
1 branch of fresh thyme (*½ teaspoon dried thyme may be substituted; Ed.*)
1 branch of fresh tarragon (*½ teaspoon dried tarragon may be substituted; Ed.*)
1 bay leaf
1 fresh sage leaf (*¼ teaspoon dried sage may be substituted; Ed.*)
10 sprigs parsley
1 leek, green leaves only
5 white peppercorns, slightly crushed
1 small dried red pepper, crumbled
3 coriander seeds
2 star anise pods
2 cloves
3 quarts cold water
2 heaping tablespoons coarse salt

PREPARATION:

Cut carrots and celery into *julienne* strips about 2 inches long. Place them in a large casserole, or kettle, with the sliced onions and shallots.

Separate the garlic cloves, but leave them unpeeled. Pierce each clove with the point of a knife, then add to the casserole.

Wrap the herbs in the green leaves of the leek and tie them together with a string. Tie the remaining spices in a small sack of cheesecloth. Place the herbs and spices in the casserole, add water, and salt.

Slowly bring the liquid to a rolling boil, then boil, continuously, for 4 minutes.

This *court-bouillon* may now be used in two ways:
    (1) For cooking fish.
    (2) Using only the vegetables, drained, as *garniture*, moisten them with white wine (preferably a Sancerre), and make a *liaison* by beating in small pieces of butter over high heat.

Both aspects of this recipe may be used for poached crayfish, scallops, shrimp, or fish.

⚜ Crème fraîche

Crème fraîche *has the consistency of voluminous, lightly whipped cream. It is excellent for sauces because it thickens more quickly than our regular heavy cream, with little chance of curdling. However, for many recipes in this book* crème fraîche *or heavy cream may be used interchangeably. Ed.*

To make 1 quart *crème fraîche*:
   4 cups heavy cream, in all (do not use ultra-pasteurized cream!)
   1 tablespoon buttermilk

   PREPARATION:

Pour 3 cups heavy cream into a large screw-top jar, add the buttermilk, then the fourth cup of cream. Tilt the jar back and forth a few times to distribute the buttermilk (or stir with a table knife), then leave the lid to the jar screwed on loosely.

   Let the cream rest in a warm place, out of reach of any draft, for the length of time necessary (*see Note*), then tighten the lid, and refrigerate the *crème fraîche*.

   The *crème* will keep for 1 to 2 weeks depending upon the temperature conditions when it was made.

NOTE: *There is always one uncertain factor in the preparation of* crème fraîche. *The temperature conditions will vary the length of time needed for the cream to react. The normal length of time would be about 14 to 18 hours, but in winter it can stretch to 24 hours and in summer shorten to 8 hours. In summer it is often a good idea to let the cream finish thickening in the refrigerator or, if the weather is extremely hot, to abandon the preparation entirely.*

   In winter the jar of cream can either be wrapped in a thick towel to speed the process, or it can be placed in a turned-off oven that has a gas pilot light. In the latter case, overnight should be sufficient. Ed.

Les sauces

SAUCES

Coulis de tomates
FRESH TOMATO SAUCE

To serve 4:
    2¼ pounds tomatoes
    4 tablespoons butter, in all
    1 small onion, chopped
    2 cloves garlic, unpeeled
    Bouquet garni (sprigs of thyme and parsley and a bay leaf, tied
        together)
    Salt
    Freshly ground pepper
    Sugar (*optional*)

PREPARING THE TOMATOES:

Drop the tomatoes into boiling water. Count to 10, then remove and plunge them into cold water. When they are chilled, cut out the core from the stem end, and peel them. Cut the tomatoes in half crosswise, and squeeze each half to remove water and seeds, then cut the flesh into small pieces.

COOKING THE SAUCE:

Melt 2 tablespoons of butter in a skillet, and sauté the onion, covered, for 5 minutes over low heat. Do not allow it to brown.

Add the tomatoes, whole garlic cloves, and *bouquet garni.* Season with salt and pepper and a pinch of sugar. Cook the sauce, covered, over medium heat for about 30 minutes.

Remove the garlic and *bouquet garni,* and purée the tomatoes by passing them through the fine blade of a food mill. Store in glass or ceramic container.

FINISHING THE SAUCE:

In a small saucepan, just before serving, return the sauce to a boil. Stir in the remaining 2 tablespoons of butter, cut into small pieces, and taste for seasoning.

Sauce froide pour crustacés
COLD SAUCE FOR SHELLFISH

To serve 4:
    20 crayfish shells (*see Note*)
    2 tablespoons peanut oil
    1 tablespoon cognac
    2 tablespoons dry white wine
    Coarse salt
    ¾ cup Fish Stock (*fumet de poisson,* page 20)
    2 rounded teaspoons tomato paste
    ⅝ cup heavy cream
    1 rounded teaspoon Dijon mustard
    4 teaspoons red wine vinegar
    Paprika
    Freshly ground pepper
    8 fresh tarragon leaves (*tarragon preserved in vinegar, or ¼ teaspoon dried tarragon, may be substituted; Ed.*)
    1 branch of parsley

NOTE: *If crayfish shells are unavailable, the shells from 1½ pounds medium- to large-size shrimp may be substituted with satisfactory results. Ed.*

PREPARATION:

Crush one-quarter of the shells at a time in a food processor or electric blender. Set aside.

Heat the oil in a heavy casserole and sauté the shells, stirring constantly. Allow about 5 minutes for this operation.

Deglaze the casserole with cognac, then add white wine. Stirring continuously, boil 1 minute over high heat. Then sprinkle with salt and pour in the *fumet*. Mix in tomato paste, then simmer, uncovered, for 20 minutes over low heat. Stir frequently.

Push the sauce through a sieve—or better yet, crush out the juices using the fine blade of a food mill. You should be able to extract ⅓ cup sauce. Place it in the refrigerator to chill.

FINISHING THE SAUCE:

In a small round-bottomed bowl, mix the cream with mustard, vinegar, a dash of paprika, and pepper. Add salt to taste. Using a wire whisk, incorporate the chilled sauce, little by little, into the cream. Add freshly chopped tarragon and parsley, then refrigerate until ready to serve.

This sauce is an excellent accompaniment for cold crayfish, lobster, crab, or shrimp.

Sauce digoinaise
MUSTARD SAUCE

To serve 4:
2 egg yolks, at room temperature
1 rounded teaspoon Dijon mustard
3 tablespoons lemon juice, in all
Salt
¾ cup imported French peanut oil, or best-quality imported olive oil
1 shallot, finely chopped
6 dashes Tabasco
½ bunch watercress (about ¾ cup leaves)

PREPARATION:

Choose a medium-size round bowl with a small bottom to give maximum efficiency when beating the sauce. Place the egg yolks in the bowl with the mustard, 1 tablespoon of lemon juice, and a pinch of salt. Stir briskly with a wire whisk while slowly adding the oil, a tablespoon at a time.

When the sauce has thickened, gradually incorporate the remaining lemon juice. Add more salt to taste and the shallot and Tabasco. Just before serving, chop the watercress and fold it into the sauce.

This sauce is an accompaniment for meats, cold or uncooked, and may also serve as a dressing for *céleri rémoulade* (celery root with mayonnaise sauce).

Sauce costelloise
ORANGE SAUCE

NOTE: *This sauce has a mayonnaiselike consistency and may be used for vegetables, particularly asparagus and broccoli, poached fish, and white meats. Ed.*

To serve 4:
 ½ cup imported olive oil
 ½ cup imported peanut oil
 ⅓ cup imported walnut oil
 Zests of 2 oranges, grated or minced
 ⅓ cup red wine vinegar
 ¼ teaspoon white peppercorns, slightly crushed
 3 egg yolks
 Coarse salt

PREPARATION:

Mix the 3 oils in a saucepan and warm them slightly over low heat. Do not let them actually become hot.

Drop the orange zest into a large amount of boiling water and blanch it for 5 minutes. Drain the zest in a fine sieve, then refresh it in a bowl of cold water, and drain again.

In a heavy 1-quart saucepan, preferably tin-lined copper, reduce the vinegar with the crushed peppercorns. When the vinegar barely coats the bottom of the pan, take it from the heat, and add 3 tablespoons cold water, followed by the egg yolks. Give the yolks a vigorous stir, using a wire whisk, and return the pan to very low heat. Stirring continuously, incorporate the warm oil in droplets, a few at a time.

When all of the oil has been incorporated, mix in the orange zest, and add salt to taste.

If the sauce must be prepared in advance, keep it warm in a double boiler (*bain-marie*) over warm, not hot water.

Sauce froide à la tomate pour Jean Yanne
UNCOOKED TOMATO SAUCE

To serve 4:
- 1¼ pounds tomatoes
- 1 rounded teaspoon tomato paste
- 4 teaspoons red wine vinegar
- ¼ cup imported virgin olive oil
- ½ teaspoon salt
- ¼ teaspoon freshly ground pepper
- 1 tablespoon coarsely chopped fresh tarragon (*see Note*)
- 1 to 2 tablespoons coarsely chopped parsley

PREPARATION:

Choose ripe, freshly picked tomatoes. Blanch 10 seconds in boiling water, then plunge them into cold water. When they are chilled, peel them. Cut the tomatoes in half and squeeze to remove the seeds and water.

Push the tomato pulp through a fine sieve, pressing down on it with the back of a wooden spoon. Collect the tomato purée in a bowl and refrigerate until ready to use.

SEASONING:

This must be done at the last moment to keep the oil from separating from the sauce.

Add tomato paste and vinegar to the sieved tomatoes. Mixing continuously with a wire whisk, incorporate the oil, a few drops at a time. Add salt, pepper, tarragon, and parsley.

NOTE: *If fresh tarragon is unavailable, substitute fresh basil. Otherwise, omit tarragon entirely. Do not substitute dried tarragon. Ed.*

This sauce is an accompaniment for Cold Vegetable Terrine (*terrine de légumes "Olympe,"* page 90), or cold fish.

Sauce purée d'estragon
TARRAGON SAUCE

To serve 4:
 6 ounces spinach, about 10 ounces before removing stems
 1¾ ounces fresh tarragon leaves, about 3 cups loosely packed (*see Note*)
 Salt
 1 cup Chicken Stock (*fond blanc de volaille,* page 16)
 30 white peppercorns (½ teaspoon), crushed
 2 tablespoons butter

HAVE READY:

1. The spinach: Remove stems and strip off the central vein of the leaves, working from bottom to top, then wash well in several changes of water.

2. The tarragon: Use freshly cut tarragon. Pull off all leaves and discard the stalks and stems.

NOTE: *In France, fresh herbs are sold in large bunches, the way we buy bouquets of flowers. Since, unfortunately, we can't buy herbs in this manner, be forewarned that one needs about 5 healthy tarragon plants to complete this recipe. However, if necessary, the quantity of tarragon may be decreased to 1 ounce, about 1¾ cups leaves, without causing the sauce to suffer. Do not in any circumstance use dried tarragon. Ed.*

COOKING:

Drop the spinach into a casserole of boiling salted water and cook 3 minutes, uncovered. Then drain and plunge it into cold water. When chilled, drain again.

Place the tarragon in a sieve and soak it 1 minute in boiling salted water. Then refresh the tarragon immediately under cold running water.

In a small casserole, bring the chicken stock to a boil. Add freshly crushed peppercorns, then tarragon. Boil rapidly, uncovered, until the liquid barely covers the bottom of the casserole; then add the spinach for just long enough to reheat.

TO FINISH:

Turn the spinach and tarragon into a fine sieve, pressing down hard on them with a wooden spoon (*a food mill may also be used; Ed.*) and catching the purée in a small bowl. Most of the leaves should manage to pass through the sieve (*or food mill*). Scrape the bottom of the sieve well with the back of a knife. (*There should be about 1½ cups of purée. Ed.*)

Heat the butter in a heavy saucepan. When it begins to brown, quickly whisk in the tarragon-spinach purée. Hold the pan over the heat just until the sauce has warmed. Do not allow it to boil. Taste for seasoning; it may need salt.

This sauce is to be served mainly with white meats and with eggs.

Sauce Albert Prost
FENNEL AND PARSLEY SAUCE

To serve 4:
 1 fennel bulb with leaves
 1½ ounces parsley leaves, about 2 cups
 1½ tablespoons butter
 2 shallots, finely chopped
 2 tablespoons dry white wine
 1 cup *crème fraîche* (page 22)
 Coarse salt
 Freshly ground pepper, preferably white
 1 scant tablespoon lemon juice

PREPARATION:

Trim the fennel bulb, reserving all young leaves. For this recipe, take only the very heart of the bulb, about 4 ounces, and dice it into a *mirepoix*.

Remove all stems from the fennel and parsley leaves. Chop the leaves together until they are completely minced. When you are finished, they should be full of moisture.

COOKING:

Melt the butter in a small saucepan and add the shallots. Cook them over low heat, covered, until they are soft but not browned.

Add the *mirepoix* of fennel and stew 8 minutes, covered, over very low heat. Stir frequently. Deglaze the pan with white wine, then reduce the liquid until the pan is nearly dry. Remove the fennel and set aside.

Pour in the *crème fraîche*, bring the sauce to a boil, and add a good pinch of salt. Boil gently for several minutes, or until thickened.

Add the minced fennel and parsley, which will give the sauce a lovely pistachio color. Season with a few turns of the pepper mill, taste for salt, and stir in the lemon juice.

Refine the sauce by putting it through a food mill, using the finest blade. Return the reserved *mirepoix* of fennel to the sauce and, over low heat, simmer a minute or two longer, then taste again for seasoning.

Serve the sauce hot (*keep it warm in a double boiler; Ed.*) or cold (*see Note*).

NOTE: *Stir in another tablespoon or two of* crème fraîche *if you want a milder sauce. The sauce seems to improve in flavor after resting a day in the refrigerator and it is also good cold. Serve as an accompaniment to fish or white meats. Ed.*

Les pâtes

PASTRY RECIPES

Pâte à foncer fine
YEAST PASTRY DOUGH

To make enough yeast dough to line a 10-inch tart ring:
- 2 cups flour, in all
- 1 tablespoon sugar (*see Note*)
- ½ teaspoon salt (*see Note*)
- 10 tablespoons butter
- ⅝ cup lukewarm milk
- One ¼-ounce package dry yeast
- 2 egg yolks

NOTE: *If this is to be used as a dessert pastry, increase the sugar to 2 tablespoons and decrease the salt to ¼ teaspoon. Ed.*

PREPARATION:

In a mixing bowl, add the sugar and salt to 1¾ cups of flour. Then blend in the butter, cut into tiny pieces, until the mixture resembles coarse meal.

Make a deep well in the center of the flour mixture and pour in the milk. Add the yeast to the milk and let it dissolve, stirring the yeast once or twice with the point of a knife.

When the yeast has completely dissolved, add the egg yolks and, little by little, work the flour into the ingredients in the well. When

31

sufficiently combined, scrape the dough out of the bowl onto a heavily floured work surface. (Use the remaining ¼ cup of flour for this.)

Knead briefly and, as soon as you are able to form a smooth ball, wrap the dough in wax paper, weight it down with a plate, and chill until ready to use.

Pâte sucrée
SWEET PASTRY DOUGH

To make 1¼ pounds sweet pastry dough:
  1¾ cups (9 ounces) flour
  6 tablespoons softened butter
  8 tablespoons sugar
  ¼ teaspoon salt
  4 egg yolks
  2 tablespoons water

PREPARATION:

Place the flour in a bowl and make a well in the center. Cut the butter into small pieces and mix it with the sugar and salt in the well. Add the egg yolks, two at a time, thinning each addition with 1 tablespoon of water.

Gradually work the flour into the egg yolks and butter. When you are satisfied that they are sufficiently blended, knead the dough twice.

Wrap the pastry in a plastic bag and, before using, chill well in the refrigerator.

Pâte feuilletée
PUFF PASTRY

NOTE: *The basic rule for puff pastry is to maintain a ratio of 1 pound butter to 1 pound flour.*

The Troisgros' recipe is no exception. However, because of differences between our butter and flour and those used in France, it is neces-

sary to change the method of preparation. In this case, I have substituted a proven recipe of my own, incorporating some helpful
suggestions the Troisgros have offered.

The two main differences in preparation are: (1) that we must
combine cake flour with our regular flour to achieve a finer texture,
and (2) that we must incorporate a portion of flour with the butter
to compensate for the higher water content in our product. Ed.

To make 2½ pounds puff pastry dough:
    2½ cups unbleached flour
    ¾ cup cake flour
    1 pound chilled, sweet unsalted butter
    2 teaspoons salt
    1 cup ice water

A marble surface is always preferable when working with puff paste,
especially in summer, when it is important to keep the dough cold.

THE DOUGH (*la détrempe*):

In a mixing bowl, combine the two flours. Remove ½ cup and set
aside.

Cut ¼ pound (1 stick) of butter into tiny pieces. Using a pastry
blender, cut the butter into the flour until the mixture resembles
coarse meal.

Dissolve the salt in the ice water, and add it to the flour, ½ cup
at a time. With a cupped hand, scoop the flour into the water until
both are mixed well enough to turn out onto your work surface.

Working quickly, with the aid of a metal spatula, or pastry scraper,
bring the dough together to form a ball. Knead once or twice, dust
with flour, and wrap in a piece of wax paper. Refrigerate 1 hour.

THE BUTTER (*le beurre*):

Place the remaining ¾ pound cold butter between two sheets of plastic
wrap. Tap it with a rolling pin in order to soften the consistency without destroying its body. As soon as the butter is malleable, discard the
plastic and, kneading with the palm of your hand, work in the reserved ½ cup of flour, a little at a time. Keep the butter firm and mold
it into a square package.

Lightly flour the work surface and roll the chilled dough into a
circle large enough to enclose the butter completely (about 12 inches

in diameter). Place the butter in the center, and bring up the dough, making sure all sides overlap slightly when they meet. Lightly tap down the dough to make a rectangular shape.

THE TURNS (*les tours*):

To give a turn is to lengthen a square of dough to a band, then fold it into 3 parts as for a business letter. Your hands should apply even pressure on the rolling pin when flattening the dough, and always roll in the same direction.

To give a turn: Rest the rolling pin in the center of the dough and push it away, reducing half the thickness. Return the rolling pin to its place of departure, without rolling it backward, then roll the remaining half of the dough toward you. Always starting from the center, repeat this procedure until the dough is reduced to a thickness of about ¾ inch, then fold it into thirds as for a letter.

At this stage the dough is called a *pâton*, meaning a piece of pastry.

The first turn being finished, follow with the second, placing the folded side of the dough on your right. Proceed as for the first turn. Then wrap the *pâton* in wax paper and place it in a plastic bag to keep it moist. Chill the dough 1 hour in the refrigerator.

After 1 hour, proceed with turns 3 and 4, rolling the dough out onto a floured surface as before. The rectangle should be consistently about 5 inches by 14 to 16 inches. After completing the two turns, return the dough, folded, to the refrigerator.

After 2 hours, complete final turns 5 and 6. At this point the dough may be cut into smaller portions, as designated for specific recipes, and refrigerated or frozen. Do not plan to use the pastry before a rest of several hours or, preferably, overnight, in the refrigerator.

When using frozen puff pastry, thaw the dough overnight in the refrigerator, not at room temperature.

Pâte à choux
CREAM PUFF PASTRY

To make 8 large pastries:
- 1 cup water
- 1 teaspoon salt
- 1 teaspoon sugar (omit sugar if the pastry will not be used for a dessert)
- 4 tablespoons butter
- 1 cup (4 ounces) flour
- 4 eggs

PREPARATION:

Pour the water into a large saucepan. Add salt, sugar, and butter, cut into tiny pieces. Slowly bring the water to a boil and, as soon as the butter is melted (*the two should happen simultaneously; Ed.*), add the flour all at once.

Using a wooden spoon, work the dough vigorously over high heat; stir constantly until it becomes a dry mass and can be pulled away from the sides of the pan. This should take about 1 minute.

Remove the pan from the heat and make a well in the center of the dough. Add the eggs, one at a time, mixing until they are thoroughly incorporated. The dough is now ready to use.

To make the *choux*, pipe the dough through a pastry bag, using a ¾-inch round tube opening, onto a buttered baking sheet.

COOKING:

Preheat oven to 425° F.

Bake the *choux* until they have puffed to double their original size (about 15 minutes), then lower the oven heat to 375° F., and continue baking until they are crisp and lightly browned.

NOTE: *If you wish to prepare the dough several days before baking, wrap it in a sheet of aluminum foil and refrigerate.*

The finished pastries may be frozen. When it is time to use them, thaw and crisp in the oven at a low temperature setting. Ed.

Les potages

SOUPS

Crème de grives à la tuilière
THRUSH SOUP

To serve 4:
    8 thrush (*see Note*)
    Coarse salt
    Freshly ground pepper
    1 tablespoon olive oil
    2 tablespoons rice
    2 thick slices white bread
    5 tablespoons butter, in all
    1 small carrot, finely chopped
    1 shallot, chopped
    Bouquet garni (sprigs of thyme and parsley and a bay leaf, tied
        together)
    6 juniper berries, crushed
    1 quart Chicken Stock (*fond blanc de volaille,* page 16)
    1¼ cups *crème fraîche* (page 22)

NOTE: *Thrush cannot be purchased in this country, but very small squab, or quail, may be substituted with excellent results. If squab are quite large, 4 will be sufficient. In most cases, one can disregard the following directions for hanging and cleaning the birds, as squab, particularly, will normally be purchased ready to cook. In either case, reserve only the heart and liver and sauté them with the carcasses. Ed.*

Soups

HAVE READY:

1. The thrush: Choose 8 thrush that have been hung. The more delicate are the redwing (*mauvis*) or those that feed on grapes (*vendangeuses*).

Pluck the birds, remove the beak and feet, and take out only the gizzard (the hard ball that one feels in the interior of the breast cavity). Extract it with the help of a trussing needle or skewer.

Using a sharp boning knife, remove the 2 breast fillets from each bird and cut them into thin slices. Marinate them until cooking time in a bowl with salt, pepper, and olive oil.

2. Place the rice in a sieve and wash it well under running water to remove the starch.

3. The croûtons: Cut the bread into ½-inch cubes. Shortly before serving, brown them in 2 tablespoons of butter.

COOKING:

Melt 1½ tablespoons of butter in a casserole and add the carcasses of the birds. Brown them well, turning them on all sides. After 10 minutes, add the *mirepoix* of carrot and shallot. Cover the casserole and cook over low heat for 10 minutes to release their juices.

Add the rice, *bouquet garni*, and juniper berries to the casserole; moisten with chicken stock and simmer 40 minutes, partially covered.

Using a skimmer, lift out the carcasses and vegetables. Cut up the carcasses with poultry shears, or a meat cleaver, and grind everything coarsely in a food processor, blender, or meat grinder. Then refine the mixture in a food mill, using the fine blade. Scrape the underside of the food mill periodically to remove the purée, and return everything you are able to extract to the broth in the casserole. (*This is a difficult and tedious task and do not expect to grind the bones to a pulp. The point is to capture all the juices and meat remaining on the carcasses as best as possible. Ed.*)

Stir in the *crème fraîche*, bring to a boil, and taste for seasoning.

Heat the remaining butter in a skillet until it sizzles and quickly sauté the sliced fillets on each side, allowing about 20 seconds in all.

TO SERVE:

Pour the boiling soup into a heated tureen.

Arrange the *garniture* of fillets with the croûtons on a warm platter and pass them separately.

Crème de pétoncles
CREAM OF SCALLOP SOUP

To serve 4:
>   2¼ pounds live *pétoncles* (*bay scallops or other shellfish; see Note*), in their shells
>   ½ cup dry white wine
>   ¾ cup Fish Stock (*fumet de poisson*, page 20)
>   1 shallot, chopped
>   1 branch fresh thyme (*or substitute ½ teaspoon dried thyme; Ed.*)
>   Coarse salt
>   2 egg yolks
>   Freshly ground pepper, preferably white
>   ¾ cup *crème fraîche* (page 22)
>   2 tablespoons chopped chives

NOTE: *Mussels or sea scallops may replace the bay scallops* (pétoncles). *If sea scallops are used, they should be halved, or quartered, depending on their size. Since both bay scallops and sea scallops are usually sold shucked in the United States, one pound will be sufficient. Ed.*

PREPARATION OF THE SCALLOPS:

Scrub the scallops well, without allowing them to soak. (*If they are already shucked, rinse them briefly. Ed.*)

Select a large heavy casserole, and add the wine, fish stock, shallot, thyme, and a good pinch of coarse salt. Cover the casserole tightly and place it over high heat. Boil for 5 minutes, then add the scallops (*with or without their shells; Ed.*), and cook them, covered, for 2 minutes. Cool the scallops before cleaning them. (*If they are already shucked, drain them immediately, reserving the broth. Ed.*)

Detach the morsel of white meat by passing a knife through the bottom of the deeper shell. (The top shell will have detached itself during the cooking.) Reserve only the white part, and the coral, and cut off the surrounding dark vein which is the intestinal tract.

Strain the cooking liquid through a sieve.

PREPARATION OF THE SOUP:

1. The *liaison*: In a small bowl, beat the 2 egg yolks with a fork and incorporate 4 to 6 tablespoons of strained broth. Add a generous amount of freshly ground pepper and set the *liaison* aside.

2. The cream: In a heavy casserole, bring the *crème fraîche* to a boil. When it is greatly reduced and quite thick, add the remaining reserved broth from the scallops, and simmer for 3 to 4 minutes.

FINISHING THE SOUP:

Off heat, or over the lowest heat possible, stir the egg-yolk *liaison* into the soup a little at a time. Using a wooden spoon, stir constantly until the soup is the consistency of light cream.

TO SERVE:

Place the scallops in the bottom of a hot soup tureen, or divide them among individual soup plates. At the last moment, chop the chives, and scatter them over the scallops. Pour the hot soup over them and serve at once.

Potage aux cosses de petits pois
YOUNG PEA SOUP

To serve 4:
    1 pound small young peas, unshelled
    4 leeks, well washed
    7 tablespoons butter, in all
    Bouquet garni (sprigs of thyme and parsley and a bay leaf, tied
        together)
    Salt
    Freshly ground pepper, preferably white
    1 small yellow heart of Boston or butter lettuce
    7 tablespoons *crème fraîche* (page 22)

PREPARATION:

Choose small young peas, freshly picked in the morning and, if possible, slightly sweet. Shell them at the last moment and reserve the shells.

Cook the peas *à l'anglaise*—dropped into rapidly boiling salted water for 2 minutes. Drain, and refresh them in a basin of ice water. When chilled, drain again, and set aside.

Coarsely chop the leeks and cook them in 4 tablespoons of butter, covered, over very low heat. Allow about 15 minutes for them to release their juices. Stir occasionally to make sure they do not brown.

Add the pea pods, stir again, and moisten with 1 quart cold water. Add the *bouquet garni*, salt, and pepper, and bring the liquid to a simmer. Cook, covered, 1 hour.

Place a food mill over a deep bowl, and in it purée the pea pods and leeks, in small quantities at a time, moistening them with the broth. Extract as much of the liquid and pulp as possible, discard the remnants, and purée again. (*Be sure to scrape the bottom of the food mill from time to time with the back of a knife. Ed.*)

FINISHING THE SOUP:

Return the puréed vegetables and broth to the casserole and bring to a boil. Shred the lettuce and add it to the soup. Stirring continuously, boil gently for 1 minute. Add the *crème fraîche* and, stirring constantly, reheat the soup to just below the boiling point, then remove from heat.

Off heat, whisk in the remaining butter, a little at a time, to give the soup body. Taste for seasoning and add the reserved peas as a *garniture*. (If the peas are lacking in sweetness, add a pinch of sugar.) Serve at once.

Potage de flageolets aux foies de volaille
CHICKEN LIVER AND BEAN SOUP

To serve 4:
>½ pound dried *flageolets* or other dried white beans, or ¾ pound
>>shelled fresh white beans
>12 chicken livers
>4 slices firm white bread (*see Note*)
>6 tablespoons butter, in all
>3 leeks, white part only, thinly sliced
>1½ quarts Chicken Stock (*fond blanc de volaille*, page 16)
>½ cup heavy cream
>Salt
>Freshly ground pepper, preferably white

HAVE READY:

1. The beans: If the beans are fresh, shell them. If they are dried, soak them for 2 hours in warm water.

2. The chicken livers: Choose the palest livers possible; they are called *foies blonds*. Divide them in two, removing any green parts and filament. Reserve 4 of the livers and cut them into ½-inch pieces.

3. The croûtons: Remove the crust from the bread and cut the slices into the smallest dice possible without their falling apart to crumbs. In a medium-size skillet, sauté the diced bread in 1 tablespoon of butter until crisp and golden brown. (*If the butter is insufficient and begins to scorch before the croûtons are done, add a little olive oil to the pan. Ed.*)

NOTE: *I suggest that you double the quantity of croûtons. They are a perfect accompaniment to the soup and are consumed faster than one would expect. Ed.*

COOKING:

Fresh *flageolets* are essentially a green vegetable and should be treated as such. Drop them into a kettle of boiling salted water and cook, uncovered, for 25 minutes.

If you are using dried beans, boil them very gently for 2 hours. Set aside ½ cup of the cooked beans.

Melt 2 tablespoons of butter in a heavy casserole, and in it sauté the leeks, covered, for 10 minutes over low heat to release their juices. When the leeks have softened, add the 8 whole livers, and cook them on both sides until firm. Allow about 10 minutes for this. Then, add the chicken stock, cover the casserole, and maintain the soup at the lowest possible simmer for 25 minutes.

Cut the reserved ½ cup of beans in half lengthwise, and set them aside. Add the rest of the beans, drained, to the soup, and pass it all through a food mill into a clean casserole.

Add the cream and bring the soup to a simmer. Taste for seasoning.

FINISHING THE SOUP:

Heat 1 tablespoon of butter in a small skillet and sauté the reserved diced livers for about 2 minutes. Season them with salt and pepper and place in the bottom of a heated soup tureen with the reserved beans.

Incorporate the remaining butter into the hot soup, little by little, stirring briskly with a wire whisk. When the soup has thickened slightly, pass it through a fine sieve (*optional*) into the tureen with the liver and beans.

It is best to serve the croûtons separately, as they should be added to the soup at the last moment in order to remain crisp.

Soup aux amandes
ALMOND SOUP

To serve 6:
    ½ pound almonds, shelled
    5 eggs
    1 quart Chicken Stock (*fond blanc de volaille*, page 16)
    3 cups *crème fraîche* (page 22)
    Coarse salt
    Freshly ground pepper, preferably white
    Sliced almonds or croûtons (*optional*)
    Butter

HAVE READY:

1. The almonds: Drop the almonds into boiling water for 1 minute. Drain them in a sieve, and slip off their skins by pinching them with your fingers.

2. The eggs: Carefully lower the eggs into boiling salted water. Cook 9 minutes, then refresh them in ice water. When they have chilled, shell them, and separate the whites from the yolks. Reserve the whites for another use.

3. Pulverize the almonds and the egg yolks together, a little at a time, in a food processor or blender. Blend until they form a smooth paste. (*The texture and consistency will be somewhat like brown sugar. Ed.*)

4. Sauté a few sliced almonds, or croûtons, in a little butter until golden. Sprinkle with coarse salt and keep warm.

COOKING THE SOUP:

Warm the chicken stock in a casserole, but do not let it actually become hot.

Off heat, stir in the *crème fraîche*, little by little, mixing until smooth. Then, incorporate the almond-egg-yolk *liaison*, 1 or 2 tablespoons at a time.

Stirring continuously with a wooden spoon, bring the soup to a boil over moderate heat. Then reduce heat to barely a simmer and cook 5 more minutes. During this time, continue to stir the soup. It will thicken and become smooth.

Taste for seasoning, adding salt, a generous amount of freshly ground white pepper and, at the last moment before serving, a *garniture* of sliced almonds or croûtons.

Soupe de carpe
CARP SOUP WITH FRESH HERBS

To serve 6 or 8:
  1 live carp, about 3½ pounds (*see Note*)
  1 onion, sliced
  Bouquet garni (sprigs of thyme and a bay leaf, tied together)
  2 cloves unpeeled garlic, crushed slightly
  Coarse salt
  1 pound spinach
  14 ounces sorrel
  3½ ounces parsley (1 large bunch)
  3½ ounces chervil (1 large bunch)
  3½ ounces watercress (1 bunch)
  10 large fresh tarragon leaves
  4 tablespoons butter, in all
  2 cups *crème fraîche* (page 22) or heavy cream
  Freshly ground pepper
  Flour
  Oil for frying

NOTE: *Carp is a freshwater "bottom" fish, particularly abundant in the Middle West and Eastern areas of the United States. Though it can be found in a multitude of ethnic fish markets, including Chinese, Scandinavian, and Jewish, I find the fish, whether live or not, only as good as the mud that it comes from. It is an oily, dark-meat fish—a kind of cross between trout and mackerel—and, at its best, the flesh can be delicate and very sweet.*

If you wish, saltwater fish or other freshwater fish may be used in place of carp. However, you may dispense with frying the boneless garniture.

This is an excellent soup for spring and fall when live carp is prevalent, and sorrel, a perennial in home gardens, is abundant. Ed.

HAVE READY:

1. The carp: Have the carp cleaned and filleted and the skin removed. Save the head, bones, and trimmings for the fish *fumet*.

Reserve the two flat, boneless parts of the body next to the stomach. Cut these into small medallions about 1¼ inches in diameter.

2. The fish *fumet*: Place all the trimmings, including the head and bones, in a small casserole. Add the onion, *bouquet garni*, garlic, 1½ quarts of cold water, and a good pinch of coarse salt. Bring the water to a boil and skim the surface. Continue to boil gently, for 25 minutes, then strain through a fine sieve.

3. The herbs: Remove the stems from the spinach, sorrel, parsley, chervil, watercress, and tarragon. Strip off the central vein from the spinach and sorrel. Wash the greens and herbs, drain well, then chop coarsely to decrease their volume and make them more manageable.

COOKING:

Rub a large heavy casserole liberally with butter. Place the thick fillets from the back of the carp in the casserole together with all the herbs and greens. Dot with the rest of the butter, cover, and cook over very low heat for 15 minutes to release the juices. (*Check midway through this operation to make sure that the greens and herbs on the bottom of the casserole do not scorch. Ed.*)

Pour the strained fish stock into the casserole and bring it to a boil. Re-cover the casserole and cook the soup for 40 minutes over moderate heat.

Pass all the soup, including the fish, through a food mill into a clean casserole. Add the *crème fraîche* and return the soup to a boil, then add pepper and taste for seasoning. (*It will probably need salt and, de-pending on the tartness of the sorrel, you may wish to add a squeeze of lemon juice. Ed.*)

TO SERVE:

Two minutes before serving the soup, heat a little oil in a small skillet. Dust the carp medallions lightly with flour, and fry them, on both sides, in very hot oil. They should brown almost instantly. Drain this *garniture* on paper towels and sprinkle with salt.

Serve the soup in hot soup bowls and the fried medallions separately on small plates. (*Although the Troisgros do not suggest serving this soup cold, by chance I found it very interesting served chilled the following day. Ed.*)

Soupe de homards et de civelles
LOBSTER SOUP WITH BABY EELS

To serve 4:
  3½ to 4 pounds live female lobsters (2 or 3 lobsters)
  Coarse salt
  Freshly ground pepper
  3 ounces *civelles* (*baby eels; see Note*)
  3 tablespoons butter, in all
  3 tablespoons olive oil
  1 onion, finely chopped
  1 shallot, finely chopped
  1 carrot, finely chopped
  1 clove garlic, crushed
  2 tomatoes, chopped
  1 rounded teaspoon tomato paste
  Bouquet garni (sprigs of thyme and parsley)
  2 tablespoons cognac
  ½ cup dry white wine
  3 cups Fish Stock (*fumet de poisson*, page 20)
  ⅜ cup *crème fraîche* (page 22), or heavy cream

NOTE: Civelles *are transparent baby eels that come from the high seas to the rivers. If you cannot obtain them—which is likely—do not substi-*

tute any other variety of eel; this rich soup needs no other seafood addition. However, in the absence of *civelles*, small toasted *croûtons* might be a nice accompaniment. Ed.

HAVE READY:

1. The lobsters: (*To distinguish a female lobster, check the small "feelers" running along the tail. Female feelers have hairy edges while male feelers are smooth. Ed.*)

Cut up the lobsters in the following manner: Detach the claws and the tails where they meet the body shells, then split the bodies in half lengthwise and break off the small pincers. Remove the stomach (the dark ball near the head), and reserve the coral (roe), which is dark green, and the pale-green tomalley. Crack the claws and season the pieces of lobster liberally with salt and pepper.

2. Drop the eels into a casserole of boiling salted water and, when the water returns to a boil, cook them for 10 seconds, then drain immediately in a colander.

COOKING:

Melt 1½ tablespoons of butter with the oil in a large casserole over high heat. Add the pieces of lobster and turn them, using two wooden spoons, until the shells have taken on a bright red color.

Add the *mirepoix* of onion, shallot, and carrot, and cook, covered, over low heat for 5 minutes.

Add the garlic, chopped tomato, tomato paste, and *bouquet garni*, and cook all together, uncovered, over moderate heat for 5 minutes, turning the pieces of lobster over in the *mirepoix* several times.

Deglaze the casserole with cognac, let it reduce, then add the white wine and fish stock. Cover the casserole and cook the lobster for 15 minutes over low heat.

Remove the lobster and set the tail and claw pieces aside. Using a meat cleaver, break up the bodies into small manageable pieces. Place them with the small pincers in a food processor, a few at a time, and grind them into as much of a paste as possible (*see Note*). Using a rubber spatula, scrape out the container of the food processor, returning the paste and crushed shells to the soup.

NOTE: *A blender will not do a satisfactory job of grinding the shells, and the food processor will not grind them completely. It may also not grind very much of the body shells at all, except for the more pliable pincers. Do not be concerned. When the shells are broken up as much as possible, return them to the soup. The essence of the lobster will be extracted later with a food mill. Ed.*

When every bit of the lobster (*except reserved tails and claws*) has been returned to the casserole, cook the soup for another 10 minutes over moderate to high heat.

While the soup is cooking, extract the meat from the tails and claws (*snipping the shells with poultry shears simplifies this task; Ed.*). Dice the lobster meat and scatter it and the cooked eels over the bottom of a warmed soup tureen.

Blend the coral and tomalley with the remaining 1½ tablespoons of softened butter, and stir it into the soup. Add the *crème fraîche*, bring the soup to a boil, and taste for seasoning. It should be spicy.

Now strain the soup through a fine sieve or, preferably, pass it through a food mill, into a clean casserole. Press down hard to extract as much essence from the crushed lobster shells and *mirepoix* as possible. Do this a little at a time, discarding the remains of the crushed shells as you proceed.

TO SERVE:

Return the soup to a boil and pour it over the diced lobster and the eels. Serve immediately.

Soupe aux moules à la feuille de thym
MUSSEL SOUP WITH FRESH THYME

To serve 4:
 2½ pounds mussels
 ½ cup dry white wine
 ¼ cup olive oil
 1 onion, finely chopped
 1 leek (white part only), finely chopped
 1 carrot, minced
 1 clove garlic, finely chopped
 3 tomatoes, peeled (directions page 23) and chopped
 Bouquet garni (sprigs of thyme and parsley and a bay leaf, tied
  together)

2 cups Fish Stock (*fumet de poisson*, page 20)
1 teaspoon saffron threads
Coarse salt
½ cup *crème fraîche* (page 22)
Freshly ground pepper
Several sprigs of fresh thyme (*or substitute 1 tablespoon chopped parsley; Ed.*)

PREPARATION OF THE MUSSELS:

Choose large heavy mussels, alive, and full of seawater. Scrape off the beards, scrub the mussels well, and rinse them in several changes of cold water without letting them soak in it.

Put the mussels in a casserole large enough to hold twice their volume. Pour the white wine over them and cover tightly. Cook the mussels about 4 minutes, turning them once or twice.

When they have opened, let cool just long enough to be handled, then remove the shells, dropping the mussels into a small bowl. Pass the cooking liquid through a fine sieve lined with cheesecloth, and pour enough of the strained broth over the mussels to cover them completely. (*This will keep them warm and moist. Ed.*) Reserve the rest of the broth.

COOKING:

Heat the olive oil in a large casserole, and add the *mirepoix* of onion, leek, and carrot. Cook over low heat, covered, for 15 minutes without letting them brown. Stir frequently.

Add the garlic, tomatoes, and *bouquet garni*. Cook 1 minute, then pour in the reserved mussel broth and the fish stock. Bring the liquid to a boil and skim the surface. Retrieve ½ cup of hot broth, blend it with the saffron, and return it to the soup. Add salt to taste, then cover, and simmer 40 minutes.

Uncover the casserole and add the *crème fraîche*. Return the soup to a gentle boil, taste for salt, and add pepper.

TO SERVE:

Place the reserved mussels, drained, in a warmed soup tureen. Rub the sprigs of fresh thyme with your fingers, letting the leaves fall over the mussels. Retrieve any stems that should accidentally follow. Pour the boiling soup over the mussels and serve.

Les salades

SALADS

Salade d'épinards nouveaux
SALAD OF YOUNG SPINACH LEAVES

To serve 4:
    8 ounces spinach
    2 hard-cooked eggs
    1 rounded teaspoon imported *moutarde blanche*, or substitute
        Dijon mustard
    4 tablespoons lemon juice
Salt
Freshly ground pepper
    10 tablespoons imported olive oil
    ¼ pound thinly sliced bacon, diced
    2 tablespoons red wine vinegar

HAVE READY:

1. The spinach: Choose young, freshly cut spinach leaves, preferably the flat-leafed variety. Pull the stems from the spinach, and tear the leaves, against the grain, into manageable pieces. Wash them in several changes of water, drain, and dry in a towel.

2. The sauce: In a round-bottomed salad bowl, blend the hardcooked egg yolks with mustard, lemon juice, salt, and pepper. Beating rapidly with a wire whisk, slowly incorporate the oil into the yolk mixture.

49

3. Coarsely chop the egg whites and set them aside.

4. In a small skillet, brown the bacon, then remove and drain on paper towels. Pour the excess fat from the skillet, but do not clean the pan.

PREPARATION:

Mix the spinach with the dressing, tossing thoroughly, then sprinkle the egg whites and bacon over all.

Return the skillet to moderate heat and deglaze with vinegar. Just before serving, pour the boiling vinegar over the salad and toss again.

Salade de faisanes
PHEASANT SALAD

(Color picture 3)

To serve 4:
  2 pheasants
  2 tablespoons butter
  3 cloves garlic, unpeeled
  1 branch of fresh thyme (*or substitute ½ teaspoon dried thyme; Ed.*)
  1 rounded teaspoon Dijon mustard
  Coarse salt
  Freshly ground pepper
  ¼ cup red wine vinegar
  ½ cup walnut oil
  2 young heads of chicory (*use only the yellow hearts; Ed.*)
  2 tomatoes
  Stale crust of a round loaf of French bread
  32 freshly shelled walnut halves

PREPARATION OF THE PHEASANTS:

Choose young pheasants, as little damaged by shot as possible, and not gamy. The weight of each, with plumage, should not exceed 2 pounds. Pluck, clean, singe, and truss the birds.

Preheat oven to 350° F.

Melt the butter in a heavy cast-iron casserole large enough to hold the birds side by side without touching. Arrange them in the casserole, and cook slowly, over medium to low heat, until they are golden brown on all sides; turn them frequently.

Add 2 unpeeled garlic cloves and the branch of thyme, cover the casserole, and place in the oven for 30 to 40 minutes, depending on the weight of the birds. Turn them periodically to brown them on all sides during the roasting, and add a little water each time they are turned in order to obtain substantial brown juices. When the pheasants are done, remove them from the casserole and set aside.

Let the casserole juices cool slightly, so that the fat will rise to the surface and can be more easily removed. Then, reduce the skimmed juices to a scant ½ cup, and pass them through a sieve, pressing down hard on the garlic.

PREPARATION OF THE SALAD (do this while the pheasants are cooking):

1. The *vinaigrette* sauce: Mix the mustard in a salad bowl with salt, pepper, and vinegar. Stirring with a wire whisk, incorporate the walnut oil a little at a time.

2. The lettuce: Separate the leaves of chicory and wash them well. Shake, and dry them in a towel.

3. The tomatoes: Drop the tomatoes into boiling water, count to 10, then remove, and plunge them into cold water. Peel the tomatoes, cut them in half, and remove the seeds. Then squeeze lightly to remove excess water. Cut them into quarters and set aside, lightly seasoned with 2 tablespoons of *vinaigrette*.

4. The crust or *chapons*: Rub the bread crust with the remaining clove of garlic, peeled. Then cut the crust into small slices the thickness of a coin, and moisten them on the inside with a drop of walnut oil. (*It is the hard crust that you want, not the bread; shave it from all sides of the loaf. Ed.*)

CARVING THE PHEASANTS:

Untruss the birds, cut away the 2 breast fillets from each, and take off the skin. The wings and legs should be saved for use as *salmis* (*a* ragoût *of game using meat that has been previously roasted; Ed.*).

Cut the breast meat into thin slices about 2½ inches long. Arrange them on a plate and brush each one with the strained juices, slightly warmed.

TO SERVE:

Mix the chicory with the *vinaigrette* and divide it among 4 large plates. Lay the slices of pheasant on top of the chicory, alternating them harmoniously with the tomatoes, walnuts, and *chapons*.

At the last moment before serving, brush the pheasant meat again with the slightly warmed juices and serve at once.

NOTE: *While the elegance of this salad lies in its being prepared with pheasant, there is no reason why it would not also be a fine dish made with guinea hen or chicken. Ed.*

Salade nouvelle
SPINACH AND DUCK LIVER SALAD

To serve 4:
    10 ounces duck livers (*see Note*)
    8 ounces young spinach leaves
    2 hard-cooked egg yolks
    1 rounded teaspoon imported *moutarde blanche,* or substitute Dijon mustard
    Juice of ½ lemon
    Salt
    Freshly ground pepper
    ⅝ cup imported virgin olive oil
    3 tablespoons imported peanut oil
    2 tablespoons red wine vinegar

NOTE: *Duck livers can often be found sold in bulk in Chinese markets. If duck livers are unobtainable, substitute chicken livers. Ed.*

PREPARATION OF THE LIVERS:

The evening before preparing this dish, plunge the livers into a casserole of boiling salted water. Cook 1 minute, then cool, and refrigerate them in the cooking liquid. This should be done in advance so that the livers will be firm.

NOTE: *Because our duck livers tend to be smaller in size and, there-fore, cook more rapidly, remove the casserole from the heat as soon as the livers are added. After 3 minutes, add a few ice cubes to speed the cooling of the liquid. Also, if you have chicken stock at hand, it is preferable to water for cooking. This is because the livers of our ducks are not quite as flavorful as those found in France. Ed.*

PREPARATION OF THE SPINACH:

The spinach should be young and tender, taken from the center of the plant. Remove the stems and strip off the central vein of the leaves. Wash the leaves well in several changes of water, shake, and dry them between two towels.

PREPARATION OF THE SAUCE:

In a salad bowl, mash the egg yolks with the mustard, lemon juice, salt, and pepper. Stirring vigorously with a wire whisk, incorporate the olive oil little by little.

COOKING AND FINISHING THE SALAD:

Take the livers from the cold cooking liquid and separate the two lobes. Remove any traces of green as well as filament. With a sharp knife dipped into hot water, cut each piece of liver into thin slices, diagonally. Each slice should weigh about ½ ounce. Lay them on a plate and season with salt and pepper.

Preheat oven to 250° F.

Place the spinach in the salad bowl and mix with the sauce. Then divide it among 4 warmed plates.

Using two large skillets (*this is to be certain that the slices of liver do not overlap; Ed.*), heat 1½ tablespoons of peanut oil in each until it begins to smoke. Working quickly, brown the livers ½ minute on each side, then arrange them in a star pattern on top of the spinach.

Pour off the oil remaining in the skillets and deglaze each one with 1 tablespoon of vinegar. While you are doing this, place the plates of spinach and liver in the warm oven for 10 seconds.

Remove the plates from the oven and moisten each slice of liver with the back of a spoon dipped in the boiling vinegar. Serve im-mediately.

Salade de queues d'écrevisses
CRAYFISH SALAD

NOTE: *Live crayfish are usually available only in limited areas of the United States. Shrimp may be substituted with success. Ed.*

To serve 4:

80 live crayfish, about 8 pounds (*or substitute 1½ pounds me-dium- to large-size shrimp in their shells; Ed.*)

Court-bouillon (page 20)

Cold Sauce for Shellfish (*sauce froide pour crustacés*, page 24)

20 tender leaves of chicory (*preferably from the delicate yellow center; Ed.*)

2 tablespoons cooked lobster roe (page 55), or paprika may be substituted

PREPARATION:

Clean and cook the crayfish (*or shrimp*) according to directions given for Crayfish Casserole (*cassolette de queues d'écrevisses*, page 69). Cool, and chill them in the refrigerator.

Reserve 4 pieces, unshelled, for decoration, and mix the remaining crayfish tails with the Cold Sauce for Shellfish.

TO SERVE:

Mound the crayfish salad on 4 individual plates and surround it with leaves of chicory. Sprinkle with either lobster roe or paprika, and decorate each plate with a single whole crayfish.

Salade riche
FOIE GRAS AND CRAYFISH SALAD WITH TRUFFLES

To serve 4:

4 ounces *foie gras*, cooked in a *terrine* (*see Note*)

24 live crayfish (*see Note*)

Court-bouillon (page 20)

The lettuces (*see Note*):

1 small Bibb lettuce
1 heart of a Boston or butter lettuce
A few leaves of red lettuce
1 yellow heart of chicory
1½ ounces truffles
Coarse salt
Juice of ¼ lemon
⅜ cup walnut oil
Lobster roe (*see Note*)
2 hard-cooked eggs
1 rounded teaspoon imported *moutarde blanche,* or substitute Dijon mustard
3 tablespoons red wine vinegar
Freshly ground pepper

NOTE: *If fresh, cooked goose liver is not available, it may be purchased in tins weighing 7¼ ounces, or more. It is usually referred to as* foie gras en bloc *and contains an attractive morsel of truffle.*

If live crayfish are not obtainable, substitute large shrimp, cooking them in the manner described for the crayfish. However, after they have been cleaned, cut them in half lengthwise so that they may better absorb the vinaigrette.

When choosing the lettuce, the importance lies in its being of as interesting a variety as possible. Be flexible with what is available.

If lobster roe (the eggs from a female lobster) is unobtainable, the Troisgros suggest creating an attractive touch of red with finely diced tomato. I found the tomato preferable. Ed.

HAVE READY:

1. The *foie gras* should be well chilled to facilitate slicing.
2. Poach the crayfish for 2 minutes in the *court-bouillon,* and clean them following the directions given on page 70.
3. Separate the lettuce leaves and wash them well, then shake, and dry them in a towel.
4. Slice the truffles paper-thin. Season them lightly with salt, lemon juice, and a little of the walnut oil.
5. Drop the lobster roe into boiling water, remove immediately, and plunge it into cold water, then drain in a sieve.
6. Peel the hard-cooked eggs, remove the yolks (save them for another use), and slice the whites into thin circles.

THE SAUCE:

Prepare the *vinaigrette* in a salad bowl. Mix the mustard with the vinegar, salt, and pepper; then, using a wire whisk, beat in the walnut oil a drop at a time, then beat the dressing until it thickens.

FINISHING THE SALAD:

Season the crayfish with several tablespoons of *vinaigrette*. Toss gently and let marinate a few minutes. Mix the lettuces with the remaining *vinaigrette*, and divide among 4 plates.

Using a sharp knife dipped repeatedly in hot water, slice the *foie gras* as thin as a coin, and lay it on top of the lettuce. Then arrange the crayfish around it.

Break the truffle slices into 3 or 4 pieces each, and arrange them on top, alternating with the sliced egg whites to form a mosaic. Separate the lobster eggs and sprinkle them over all, or create the same effect with diced tomato, well drained.

Les oeufs

EGGS

Omelette à la chiffonnade de cresson
WATERCRESS OMELETTE

To serve 4:
    1 pound watercress, about 3 bunches
    6 tablespoons butter, in all
    1 shallot, chopped
    Salt
    Freshly ground pepper
    1 clove garlic, peeled
    8 eggs

PREPARATION OF THE WATERCRESS:

Wash the watercress and remove all stems. Set aside 24 leaves for decoration.

Melt 3 tablespoons of butter in a skillet over low heat. Add the shallot and cook, covered, a few minutes to release the juice. Then add the watercress and sprinkle lightly with salt and pepper. Cover the skillet and let stew for 20 minutes over low heat. When the watercress is limp, spread it out on a cutting board and, using a large knife, chop into fine shreds.

Melt 1½ tablespoons of butter in a small saucepan and, as it begins to brown, add the watercress. Impale the clove of garlic on the tines of a fork and use it to stir the watercress. Taste for seasoning.

PREPARATION OF THE OMELETTE:

Break the eggs into a bowl, season them with salt and pepper, and carefully beat in about ¾ tablespoon of butter cut into tiny pieces.

Melt the remaining butter in a hot skillet and, when it foams, pour in the beaten eggs. Stirring rapidly with a fork, turn the cooked portions into the uncooked. Shake the pan in order to help the eggs solidify in mass and yet remain soft. When they become fluffy, raise the handle of the pan to turn part of the omelette onto its other side.

TO SERVE:

Fill the center of the omelette with the watercress, and roll the omelette, reversing it completely, onto a serving platter. Brush the surface with a morsel of softened butter to give it brilliance.

Drop the reserved watercress leaves into boiling water for 30 seconds, then drain in a sieve. Decorate the omelette with the leaves and serve immediately.

Oeufs durs Villemont
HARD-COOKED EGGS WITH RED PEPPER, ONION, AND SWISS CHARD SAUCE

To serve 4:

⅔ pound spring onions (*or use sweet "Spanish" onions; Ed.*)
½ sweet red bell pepper
1¾ ounces Swiss chard leaves (about 3 cups, shredded)
3 tablespoons butter
2 teaspoons flour
⅜ cup milk, warmed
Salt

Freshly ground pepper, preferably white
Nutmeg
½ cup *crème fraîche* (page 22)
8 eggs

HAVE READY:

1. The onions: Peel the onions and cut them in half. With a small knife, remove ¼ inch from the stem and root ends. This is for two reasons: (1) to remove any bitterness and (2) to detach the rings from one another. Cut the onions into even slices, as thin as possible. (If sweet onions are not in season, we recommend that you blanch the onion slices for 5 minutes before sautéing them.)

2. The sweet pepper: Remove the seeds and white fibers, and cut the pepper into long thin strips.

3. The Swiss chard: Wash the chard and shred it coarsely.

COOKING THE SAUCE:

Melt the butter in a heavy skillet. Add the onions, and cook 5 minutes, or until golden. Stir frequently with a wooden spoon.

Add the sweet pepper, cover the skillet, and reduce heat to low. Stew the pepper with the onions for 15 minutes, then add the Swiss chard, and continue to cook 5 minutes longer. Do not allow the chard to brown.

Sprinkle the vegetables with flour, and cook for a minute or two, stirring frequently. Slowly add the warm milk, a little at a time, stirring constantly, and stir until the flour is smoothly incorporated. Season the sauce with salt, pepper, and a suspicion of freshly grated nutmeg. Simmer 20 minutes, then add the *crème fraîche* and let the sauce come back to a gentle boil. Taste for seasoning.

PREPARE THE EGGS:

Carefully arrange the eggs in a strainer and submerge them in boiling salted water. Cook 9 minutes, then place them under cold running water until cool enough to handle. Remove the shells and drop the eggs into a bowl of lightly salted hot water.

TO SERVE:

Cut each egg in half and arrange the halves on a heatproof ceramic serving platter (eggs will tarnish a silver platter). Cover with the sauce and simmer a minute or two before serving.

Oeufs coque aux crevettes grises
SOFT-BOILED EGGS WITH SHRIMP

To serve 4:
> ½ pound tiny shrimp, cooked (preferably cooked in *court-bouillon,*
>   page 20)
> 1 teaspoon butter
> ½ shallot, chopped
> 8 fresh eggs
> 8 egg cups (*coquetiers*)
> 1 hard-crusted French roll

PREPARATION OF THE SHRIMP:

Shell and devein the shrimp and cut them each into 3 or 4 pieces the size of a grain of rice.

Melt the butter in a small saucepan, and cook the shallot over very low heat, covered, for a few minutes to bring out its essence. Add the shrimp, and cook, stirring, just long enough to warm them. Do not let them brown.

PREPARATION OF THE EGGS:

Cook the eggs in the classic manner, lowering them into boiling water for 3 to 4 minutes, depending on their size.

TO SERVE:

Using a serrated knife, tap the top quarter of each egg lightly, and as soon as the shell has been pierced, gently saw around the egg to detach a lid. Extract the white remaining inside the lid with a teaspoon and replace it with shrimp.

Rest the main portion of the eggs in their *coquetiers* and, with a quick gesture, replace the lids without letting the shrimp fall out.

Cut thin sticks (*mouillettes*) about 2½ inches long from the French roll for dipping into the eggs.

Oeufs au plat Paoli
BAKED EGGS ⚜

NOTE: *This recipe may easily be divided to serve 1 or 2 persons. Ed.*

To serve 4:
  8 fresh eggs
  Salt
  1 cup *crème fraîche* (page 22)
  4 ounces *jambon de Bayonne*, minced (*substitute Italian prosciutto; Ed.*)
  2 tablespoons butter
  Freshly ground pepper, preferably white

Preheat oven to 425° F.

HAVE READY:

1. Carefully separate the eggs, dropping 2 yolks into each of 4 small bowls. Put the whites together in a mixing bowl.

2. Add a pinch of salt and the *crème fraîche* to the whites and, with a manual eggbeater or a wire whisk, beat them together for 30 seconds. Fold in the minced ham.

3. Take 4 individual, heatproof porcelain (*or enameled cast-iron; Ed.*) egg dishes, add ½ tablespoon of butter to each, and place them in the oven until the butter is melted, but not brown.

COOKING:

Divide the egg-white mixture among the 4 dishes, and place them in the oven for 2½ minutes.

Gently pull out the oven rack, leaving the egg dishes within the warmth of the stove, and slide 2 yolks onto each bed of egg white. Give each portion a few good turns of the pepper mill (do not add salt), and return the dishes to the oven for 2½ to 3 minutes.

Serve the eggs in their dishes, but bear in mind that they will continue to cook after they leave the oven. Serve them instantly!

❧ *Oeufs pochés Bodin*
POACHED EGGS IN PASTRY SHELLS
WITH VEGETABLE PURÉE

To serve 4:

½ recipe Cream Puff Pastry (*pâte à choux*, page 35), or 4 large
pastry shells purchased from a bakery
6 ounces string beans
4 small tomatoes
Coarse salt
Sprigs of fresh thyme (*or substitute ½ teaspoon dried thyme; Ed.*)
4 eggs
3 tablespoons distilled white vinegar
2 tablespoons butter
Freshly ground pepper

HAVE READY:

1. The *pâte à choux*: Preheat oven to 425° F.

Using a pastry bag, pipe out 4 large *choux* onto a buttered baking
sheet. Bake them for 15 minutes, or until puffed and doubled in size,
then lower heat to 375° F. and continue to bake until they are lightly
browned. Keep the pastries warm in the turned-off oven, or reheat
them later, at a low temperature setting, when they are to be used.

2. The string beans: Drop the beans into a casserole of boiling
salted water. Boil rapidly for 8 minutes, uncovered. They should remain somewhat crunchy. Drain the beans in a colander, then quickly
plunge them into ice water. When they are thoroughly chilled, drain
again. Press the beans through a fine sieve or purée them in a food
mill.

3. The tomato sauce: Coarsely chop the tomatoes and put them
in a heavy saucepan with coarse salt and a few sprigs of thyme. Cook
about 20 minutes, stirring occasionally. Pass the tomatoes through a
food mill, then return the sauce to the stove. Boil, uncovered, until
thickened.

4. The poached eggs: Fill a 9- to 10-inch skillet with water and
add vinegar. Do not add salt. Bring to a boil, then lower heat to a
simmer. Break the eggs, one after the other, against the side of the
skillet, opening them as near as possible to the surface of the water,

then gently slide them in (*further suggestions page 64*). With a wooden spoon, carefully wrap the white around the yolk, then return the water to a boil. At that moment, remove the skillet from the heat, and let the eggs poach for 3 to 3½ minutes.

Using a skimmer, carefully lift the eggs from the skillet, and plunge them into a bowl of warm salted water. Set aside.

TO FINISH:

Melt 1 tablespoon of butter in a saucepan and, just as it begins to brown, stir in the string-bean purée to reheat.

Bring the tomato sauce to a boil and beat in the remaining tablespoon of butter.

Season the string beans and tomatoes with salt and pepper.

Carefully plunge the eggs into a pan of very hot, but not boiling water. Let them stand for several minutes.

TO SERVE:

Cut a lid off each *chou* and reserve it. Working quickly, fill the bottom of each pastry with a portion of string-bean purée. Place a well-drained egg on top, and nap neatly with tomato sauce.

Replace the lids and serve very hot.

Oeufs pochés et frits à la purée stéphanoise
EGGS POACHED AND FRIED ON A PURÉE OF GREEN VEGETABLES

To serve 4:
    7 eggs (5 eggs plus 2 egg yolks)
    3 tablespoons distilled white vinegar
    1½ tablespoons butter
    1½ tablespoons flour
    1¼ cups Chicken Stock (*fond blanc de volaille*, page 16)
    Salt
    Freshly ground pepper, preferably white
    ¾ cup heavy cream

2 tablespoons imported peanut oil
2 cups fine bread crumbs, freshly prepared
Oil for deep frying
Coarse salt
Purée of Four Vegetables (*purée de légumes stéphanoise*, page
    205)

NOTE: *This is a very delicate recipe—in the physical sense of poaching and handling the partially cooked eggs. If your confidence wavers, poach an extra egg or two, for insurance.*

The result of this recipe should be four separate taste sensations: the deep-fried crispness of the crumb coating, the smooth richness of the sauce surrounding the poached egg white, the pleasant surprise of warm, running egg yolk, and the contrasting fresh green taste of the vegetable purée. Ed.

PREPARATION OF THE EGGS:

Fill about three-quarters of a 9- to 10-inch skillet with 1 quart cold water and add the vinegar. Do not add salt. Bring the water to a boil, then reduce heat to barely a simmer.

Break 4 eggs, one after the other, against the side of the skillet (*see Note*). Open the eggs as near as possible to the surface of the water and smoothly slide them in. Try not to let them go askew. Poach the eggs 3 to 3½ minutes, adjusting the heat to prevent the water from returning to a boil.

NOTE: *If you are unsure of the poaching procedure, it helps first to break the egg into a small bowl. Rest the rim of the bowl on the surface of the water and gently tip the egg in. If you do this, have 4 small bowls waiting, each with an egg, so that the timing is not lost. Ed.*

Remove the eggs with a skimmer and drop them into a bowl of cold water. After a few minutes, lift them out and drain them on several thicknesses of paper towels. Using a small knife, trim off the rough edges, making neat ovals.

PREPARATION OF THE SAUCE:

Melt the butter in a heavy 1-quart saucepan over low heat. Add flour, and cook over low heat for 5 minutes, stirring constantly. Blend in the chicken stock, a little at a time. Season this *roux* with salt and pepper, and cook for 1 hour over very low heat. Stir frequently. At the end of this time the sauce will have reduced to about ½ cup.

In a small mixing bowl, beat the 2 egg yolks with the cream. Little by little, add half the sauce and, when well blended, return this mixture to the saucepan with the remaining sauce. Cook over moderate heat and stir continuously with a wire whisk until the sauce is reduced to approximately ¾ cup. Then pour it into a chilled bowl, resting over ice, and continue to stir until it is tepid. *(Because the sauce has a slight resemblance to* hollandaise, *I had the urge to add a few drops of lemon juice. Taste it and judge for yourself. Ed.)*

Taking great care, dip each egg into the sauce and coat it on all sides. Place the eggs on a sheet of wax paper and refrigerate until their coating is firm. *(A well-worn wooden spoon with soft edges will help this operation, and remember!—if an egg breaks, the yolk will run. Ed.)*

FRYING THE EGGS:

Break the remaining egg into a soup plate with the peanut oil, and beat to mix well. This is called an *anglaise.*

Using the side of a knife while lifting the wax paper, carefully detach the eggs one at a time, and turn them over once or twice in the *anglaise.* Then roll, one at a time, in bread crumbs until thoroughly covered. *(The eggs may now have a short rest before the completion of their cooking. Ed.)*

Heat the oil for frying to 360° F. in a deep-frying pan.

Using a skimmer, carefully lower the eggs, one by one, into the hot oil and, with a delicate movement of the side of the skimmer, keep the eggs rotating so as to prevent them from sticking to one another. *(The eggs will become well browned and ready for removal almost instantly. Ed.)*

Lift them out with the skimmer and drain on paper towels. Sprinkle lightly with coarse salt.

TO SERVE:

Spoon a bed of hot vegetable purée into individual heated ramekins or small, deep soup plates. Top each with a crisp hot egg and serve at once.

Oeufs pochés à la fausse coque
BROILED TOMATOES STUFFED WITH EGGS AND SPINACH

(Color picture 1)

To serve 4:
    12 oblong Italian "plum" tomatoes, about 2 pounds (3 per person)
    Salt
    Freshly ground pepper
    3 ounces spinach
    4 eggs
    7½ tablespoons butter, in all
    1 clove garlic, peeled
    12 egg cups (*coquetiers*)

HAVE READY:

1. The tomatoes: Choose long oval tomatoes. Their shape will lend itself perfectly to substituting for eggs in the *coquetiers*.

Cut ⅓ off the more pointed top of each tomato, and with a small spoon (*as small as a demitasse spoon; Ed.*) extract seeds and part of the pulp, leaving a solid shell about ¼ inch thick.

Season the interior of the tomatoes lightly with salt and pepper, then stand them upright in a casserole, or pan, just large enough to hold them side by side. (*I found a small loaf pan suitable. Ed.*)

2. The spinach: Prepare the spinach in the classic manner described on page 184. Boil 1 minute and, after having drained it, press out excess water, then chop the spinach coarsely.

3. The eggs: Separate the whites from the yolks into two bowls. Add a dash of salt to each and beat them moderately. (*Before you proceed to cook the eggs, decide on what utensils to use; see later in the recipe. Ed.*)

COOKING:

Preheat the broiler.

NOTE: *Essentially, four separate operations will now be performed simultaneously. Make sure that the short time needed for cooking is free from interruptions. Ed.*

Cut 2 tablespoons of butter into 12 small pieces and drop 1 piece inside each tomato. Place the tomatoes under the broiler for about 5 minutes, or until cooked but still firm enough to hold a filling without collapsing.

At the same time, melt 1½ tablespoons of butter in a small skillet over low heat. Impale the clove of garlic on the tines of a fork and keep it nearby. Add the spinach to the skillet and stir, moving it about with the garlic on the fork; warm the spinach thoroughly without allowing it to brown.

When the spinach is nearly ready and the tomatoes are under control (about 3 minutes before serving), melt 1 tablespoon of butter in each of 2 small heavy-bottomed saucepans, over low heat. (Use pans with heavy bottoms so that the eggs will not cook too fast. Or, cook them in small double boilers, which will take more time.)

First, add the egg whites to one of the saucepans and, over low heat, stir them continuously with a wooden spoon from the time they begin to coagulate until they form a lightly solidified mass. Remove from the heat and keep warm; they will finish cooking by themselves.

Add the egg yolks to the second saucepan, and cook them in the same manner, stirring with a wooden spoon. Then incorporate 1 tablespoon of butter, cut in tiny pieces, into both the cooked whites and yolks.

TO SERVE:

Place the 12 cooked tomatoes in the 12 egg cups, and fill four with each of the three preparations. Arrange the *coquetiers* on 4 plates—one white, one yellow, one green per plate—and serve at once.

NOTE: *The tomato stuffed with spinach is a delicious accompaniment to grilled meats. Ed.*

Les entrées

FIRST COURSES

 Bouillon d'escargots dormeurs
SNAIL BOUILLON

To serve 4:
    40 fresh snails
    Coarse salt
    7 tablespoons butter
    1 carrot, finely chopped
    1 leek, white part only, finely chopped
    1 onion, finely chopped
    1 stalk celery, finely chopped
    ½ cup dry white wine
    3 cups Chicken Stock (*fond blanc de volaille*, page 16)
    Bouquet garni (sprigs of thyme and parsley and a bay leaf, tied
       together)
    2 to 3 tablespoons coarsely chopped fresh basil or chervil

PREPARATION OF THE SNAILS (*les escargots*):

This recipe will not succeed without the variety of snails that hiberate in their shells during winter.

NOTE: *In truth, I found it preferable to enjoy this recipe with canned escargots rather than forego it. If the canned variety is substituted, three or four 4½-ounce tins, drained, will be sufficient. This will provide either 9 or 12 snails per person. Add them to the bouillon after the chicken broth, then simmer 20 minutes as directed. Ed.*

Remove the chalky seal of the snails by slipping the point of a knife underneath. Wash the snails in several changes of water and let them disgorge for 2 hours sprinkled with a handful of coarse salt.

Then place the snails in a kettle of cold water, bring to a boil, and drain immediately. Pick out their meat with a skewer or toothpick, and cut off the black part which is the intestine. Set aside.

FINISHING THE BOUILLON:

Heat 1½ tablespoons of butter in a large casserole and cook the *mire-poix* of carrot, leek, onion, and celery over low heat for 5 minutes. Stir frequently with a wooden spoon.

Deglaze the casserole with white wine and reduce, then add the chicken stock. Bring the broth to a boil and add the snails with the *bouquet garni*. Salt lightly, reduce heat, and simmer, uncovered, for 20 minutes.

Remove the snails with a slotted spoon or skimmer, and place them in a warm casserole. Discard the *bouquet garni*.

Bring the broth to a rolling boil. Add the remaining butter, cut into tiny pieces, stirring vigorously with a wire whisk. Pour the bouillon over the snails.

TO SERVE:

Divide the snails among 4 hot soup plates. Add bouillon to each, but do not submerge the snails, so that each one may be sprinkled with a few grains of coarse salt. Scatter the fresh basil, or chervil, generously over all, and serve at once. (*The herbs must be fresh. If necessary, substitute parsley. Accompany this delicate* entrée *with crusty French bread. Ed.*)

Cassolette de queues d'écrevisses
CRAYFISH CASSEROLE

To serve 4:
    80 live crayfish, about 8 pounds (*see Note*)
    2 quarts *court-bouillon* (page 20)
    ½ cup Sancerre or other dry white wine

8 tablespoons butter
Juice of ¼ lemon
4 fresh tarragon leaves, chopped
Salt
Freshly ground pepper, preferably white
1 sprig flat-leafed parsley

NOTE: *In areas of the United States where crayfish are unobtainable, substitute 1½ pounds large, uncooked shrimp. Ed.*

PREPARATION OF THE CRAYFISH:

The crayfish must be live; this is a rule without exceptions.

In a large casserole, bring the *court-bouillon* to a boil. If the crayfish are disgorged, drop them into the boiling bath, and cook them, covered, 3 minutes. (*See Note below for shrimp. Ed.*)

If they are not disgorged, proceed to clean them. That is to say, remove the intestinal tract. To do this, pierce the exterior orifice found under the middle band of the shell. Give it a quarter turn and pull lightly in order to root out all the waste matter.

We recommend that you clean 20 at a time, cook and drain them, then begin again. Repeat the operation 4 times. This is in order to avoid having the crayfish empty themselves.

When the crayfish are cooked, take them from the casserole and cool slightly. Then, slit them open, and reserve the tail meat taken from the shell.

NOTE: *If using shrimp, drop them, all at once, into boiling court-bouillon for the same length of time as the crayfish. However, for quick and easy removal without an entanglement of vegetables, tie the shrimp together in a cheesecloth bag, or use a wire basket. Then shell and clean them and set aside.*

FINISHING THE *cassolette*:

With a skimmer, retrieve the vegetable *garniture* from the *court-bouillon*, except for the garlic and *bouquet garni*. Place the vegetables in a casserole and moisten them with white wine. Reduce the liquid by half over high heat.

While the wine is still boiling, use a wooden spoon to incorporate the butter, cut into tiny pieces, forming a *liaison* the consistency of a *beurre fondu* (thickened butter sauce).

Add the crayfish, a few drops of lemon juice, and the chopped tarragon. Correct the seasoning with salt and pepper.

Let the sauce simmer for 2 minutes without reaching a boil. The dish is ready when the crayfish are hot but still retain their delicate texture.

Divide the crayfish among warmed individual casseroles and arrange the vegetable *garniture* on top. Sprinkle with parsley leaves and serve at once.

Crépazes
MOLDED HAM CRÊPES
(Color picture 9)

To serve 4:
    6 ounces *jambon cru*, thinly sliced (*see Note*)
    6 ounces *jambon blanc*, thinly sliced (*see Note*)
    1 cup *crème fraîche* (page 22), or heavy cream
    Coarse salt
    Freshly ground pepper, preferably white
    2 ounces *gruyère* cheese, coarsely grated (about ¾ cup loosely packed)

    CRÊPE BATTER:

1 cup flour
2 eggs
¼ teaspoon salt
½ cup milk
2 tablespoons melted butter

NOTE: Jambon cru, *raw ham, is not to be confused with fresh pork. In this country Westphalian ham, sold by German butchers, makes a satisfactory substitute. If it is unobtainable, use Italian prosciutto. Jambon* blanc, *white ham, may be substituted for by either Black Forest ham, sold by German butchers, or Virginia ham. Ed.*

PREPARATION OF THE CRÊPES:

Put the flour, eggs, and salt together in a mixing bowl. With a wire whisk, slowly incorporate the milk, little by little. Refine the batter by straining it through a fine sieve, then stir in the melted butter.

Heat a crêpe pan with a bottom 6 inches in diameter (or a small, heavy cast-iron skillet with curved sides) until smoking. Using scant portions of batter, prepare ten 6-inch crêpes and set them aside. (*If you should by chance find that there is enough batter for more crêpes, by all means keep going and use them all. Ed.*)

ASSEMBLING THE CRÊPES AND HAM:

In a small heavy saucepan, bring the *crème fraîche* to a boil. Remove it from the heat and add a pinch of coarse salt and a generous grinding of pepper. Stir once and set aside.

Preheat oven to 400° F.

Lightly butter the bottom and sides of a *charlotte* mold, or a similar utensil with high sides and a diameter of 6 inches.

Place a crêpe in the bottom of the mold, and make successive layers of crêpes and ham, alternating the two hams, until all the crêpes have been used. Baste each layer of ham with approximately 2 tablespoons of hot *crème fraîche*, and finish the mold with a crêpe.

COOKING:

Bake the crêpes, uncovered, for 20 minutes. While they are baking, preheat the broiler.

Unmold the pile of crêpes and ham, upside down, onto a round heat-proof serving platter or *au gratin* dish. Sprinkle the top with cheese and place under the broiler, as far from the heating unit as possible. Grill until the cheese is melted and bubbling.

Using a long bread knife, divide the *crépazes* into quarters and serve at once.

Grenouilles au blanc de blancs
FROGS' LEGS WITH CHAMPAGNE

NOTE: *Blanc de blancs is a still white wine produced from champagne grapes, therefore entitled to the term champagne. Ed.*

To serve 4:
  24 pairs of frogs' legs (*see Note*)
  Salt
  Freshly ground pepper
  Flour
  4 tablespoons butter
  2 large shallots, chopped
  ⅝ cup *champagne blanc de blancs*, or other dry white wine
  1¼ cups *crème fraîche* (page 22)
  2 cloves garlic, finely chopped
  2 tablespoons chopped parsley
  ¼ lemon

NOTE: *Frogs' legs, as found in France, are usually of considerably smaller size than those found in the United States. In this country, a dozen pairs of legs, or about 2½ pounds, will be sufficient. Because of their large size, separate each pair of legs before cooking. Ed.*

PREPARATION OF THE FROGS' LEGS (*les grenouilles*):

The best season for frogs' legs is spring. Since you can buy frogs' legs ready to cook, we won't speak of the difficult and disagreeable task of cleaning them.

Sprinkle the frogs' legs with salt and pepper and roll them in sifted flour.

Heat the butter in a large heavy skillet (*about 14 inches in diameter*). As the butter begins to color, arrange the frogs' legs in the pan, ventral side down, without overlapping. When they have browned on one side, turn them, one by one, with a two-pronged fork or tongs. (*If necessary, add a little more butter, or olive oil, during the cooking. Ed.*) When the legs are evenly browned the butter should be completely absorbed. (*Allow about 15 minutes for this operation, check the frogs' legs constantly, and take care not to let the butter burn. Ed.*) As they are finished, place them on a warm, heatproof serving platter.

PREPARATION OF THE SAUCE:

In the same skillet, sauté the shallot, covered, for 30 seconds over low heat. Deglaze the pan with the wine and, when it is reduced by three-quarters, add the *crème fraîche*. Stirring with a wire whisk, bring the sauce to a boil. Cook for 2 minutes or until the sauce is slightly thickened.

Place the platter of frogs' legs over low heat and coat them with the sauce. Scatter the chopped garlic and parsley over all, and taste for seasoning. Add salt and pepper as needed, and simmer 1 minute, spooning the sauce over the frogs' legs. Then add a squeeze of lemon juice and serve very hot.

Coffrets de ris de veau
SWEETBREADS IN PUFF PASTRY SHELLS

To serve 4:
    2 pairs sweetbreads, about 2½ pounds (*see Note*)
    1 onion, thinly sliced
    1 carrot, thinly sliced
    Bouquet garni (sprigs of thyme and parsley and a bay leaf, tied together)
    2 tablespoons dry white wine
    1 quart Chicken Stock (*fond blanc de volaille*, page 16)
    ½ pound fresh leaf spinach
    Salt
    ½ pound Puff Pastry (*pâte feuilletée*, page 32)
    1 egg
    2 tablespoons butter, in all
    1 tablespoon flour
    1 cup *crème fraîche* (page 22)
    Freshly ground white pepper
    ¼ lemon
    1 clove garlic, peeled

NOTE: *The Troisgros' original recipe calls for 1 pair of sweetbreads, weighing about 1¼ pounds. Even though the larger quantity I have recommended will overflow its pastry container, the recipe is delicious, and those who enjoy sweetbreads will have no trouble consuming this amount. Also, when they are thoroughly cleaned, their volume decreases considerably. The amount of sauce is correct for either quantity. Ed.*

PREPARATION OF THE SWEETBREADS:

Prepare the sweetbreads the day before you are to serve them. They must be very fresh, and choose the whitest possible.

1. Soak the sweetbreads 5 to 6 hours in ice water, changing the water frequently. At the end of this time, pull off all membrane, tissues, and fat that can be removed easily without causing damage to the sweetbreads.

2. Place them in a large casserole, cover with cold water and, over moderate heat, slowly bring to a simmer, uncovered. (This slow, progressive blanching will help to firm the sweetbreads.) When a simmer is reached, continue to cook gently for 5 minutes, then plunge the sweetbreads into ice water.

3. Drain and separate the lobes—the throat (*la gorge*) which is long, and the kernel (*la noix*) which is round. Carefully pull off all remaining membrane and set aside.

4. Place the onion, carrot, and *bouquet garni* in a heavy casserole large enough to hold the sweetbreads side by side. Put the sweetbreads on top of the *garniture*, sprinkle with white wine, and cook, covered, over low heat for 10 minutes to release the juices of the *garniture*. Then remove the cover and raise the heat long enough for the wine to evaporate. Add chicken stock, cover the casserole, and cook barely at a simmer for 40 minutes.

Remove the sweetbreads, cool, and refrigerate them overnight. Strain and reserve the broth.

THE SPINACH:

Wash the spinach well, strip off the stems, then cook in the classic manner described on page 184. Press out the water remaining in the leaves and set aside.

THE PASTRY SHELLS:

Preheat oven to 425° F.

The puff paste should have had all 6 turns and a good rest in the refrigerator. Roll it out into a rectangle 6 inches by 8 inches with an even thickness of about ½ inch. Divide the pastry into 4 pieces, 3 inches by 4 inches, and lay them on a baking sheet that has been moistened with cold water. Refrigerate 15 minutes.

Beat together the egg and 1 teaspoon of water in a small bowl, and brush the pastries with this. Then, with the point of a knife, draw a rectangular imprint around the top of each pastry, about ½ inch in from the edge. Do not cut completely through the dough.

Bake the shells 15 minutes, then turn off the oven. Let them remain inside 20 minutes, or longer, to dry. (*Check after 5 minutes to be sure they are not going to burn. Ed.*)

PREPARATION OF THE SAUCE:

In a casserole large enough to hold the sweetbreads side by side, melt 1 tablespoon of butter. Then add the flour, and make a *roux*, moistening it with 1 cup of the reserved, strained chicken broth. As the sauce thickens, add another ½ cup of broth, then simmer 20 minutes, stirring occasionally.

Add 1 cup *crème fraîche*, a generous grinding of pepper, and a squeeze of lemon juice. Taste for seasoning, boil 2 minutes, then remove from heat.

FINISHING THE SWEETBREADS:

1. The spinach: Over medium to low heat, melt 1 tablespoon of butter in a saucepan. Impale the clove of garlic on the tines of a fork and use it to swirl the butter, then add the spinach, and reheat it, stirring with the fork until the pan is dry.

2. The sweetbreads: Take the sweetbreads in your hands and, with your thumb and index finger, separate them into pieces naturally (*as you would a cauliflower; Ed.*), leaving the parts that tend to stay fixed together intact. Arrange the pieces in the casserole to reheat, spooning the sauce over them.

3. The pastry shells: Preheat oven to 350° F.

With the point of a small knife, cut around the pastry shells, following the imprint. Lift off the lids and reserve them. Pull out all the excess interior pastry, and dry the insides of the shells briefly in the oven.

TO SERVE:

Line the bottom of the pastry shells with spinach. Then divide the sweetbreads and sauce among them. Return the lids and serve at once.

Pass the remaining sauce separately in a hot sauceboat.

Escargots de Bourgogne poêlés
SNAILS IN BUTTER SAUCE

To serve 4:

40 fresh snails (*see Note*)
1 small carrot, sliced
½ onion, stuck with 2 cloves
1 clove garlic, unpeeled
½ cup dry white wine
10 peppercorns, crushed
Bouquet garni (sprigs of thyme and parsley and a bay leaf, tied
  together)
1½ teaspoons coarse salt

SNAIL BUTTER:

7 tablespoons butter
1 large clove garlic, minced
1 shallot, minced
¼ teaspoon coarse salt
¼ teaspoon freshly ground pepper
½ cup finely chopped parsley

PREPARATION OF THE SNAILS:

If the snails are *bouchés* or *dormeurs*, sealed or hibernating (November to March), the same preparation applies as for Snail Bouillon (page 68). If they are *coureurs*, moving and awake (March through April), let them disgorge themselves for 12 hours instead of 2 hours.

Put the shelled snails in a large casserole and add the carrot, onion, garlic, wine, pepper, and *bouquet garni*. Pour enough water over them to cover them by one-third their volume, then add 1½ teaspoons of coarse salt. Bring the liquid to a boil and, with a large spoon, remove the scum that rises to the surface. Turn the heat to very low, cover the casserole, and cook the snails 3½ hours. During this time, the liquid should, at most, barely simmer.

When the cooking is finished, remove the snails from the casserole and place them in a bowl, then strain the cooking liquid over them.

NOTE: *If fresh snails are not available, which is likely to be the case, this recipe can be adapted to the canned variety generally found in fancy-food sections of department stores and gourmet-cooking shops.*

Buy three or four 4½-ounce tins. There are usually a dozen snails to a can, so judge for yourself the number per person you think appropriate.

Heat the snails, as described, in the court-bouillon *with the aromatic vegetables,* bouquet garni, *and their canning liquor. Reduce the quantity of salt to ½ teaspoon and, if necessary, add just enough water with the wine to submerge the snails completely. Bring to a boil, then lower the heat to a simmer and cook, covered, for 30 minutes instead of 3½ hours. Ed.*

PREPARATION OF THE BUTTER:

While the snails are cooking, prepare the butter. Cut cold butter into small pieces and place it in a bowl with the garlic, shallot, salt, and pepper. Mash well with a fork, then blend in the parsley, making a smooth paste. (If not sufficiently smooth, force the butter through a sieve.) Turn the butter out onto a sheet of wax paper and divide it into small parcels.

FINISHING THE *escargots*:

Five minutes before serving, place small individual casseroles or ramekins in the oven to warm, and put the snails into a heavy casserole or saucepan on top of the stove with 4 tablespoons of their broth. Cook the snails until they are heated through, then divide them among the small casseroles.

Boil the remaining snail broth down to 1 tablespoon. Then, over high heat and using a wooden spoon, quickly stir in the snail butter, a few pieces at a time. Boil the sauce, stirring constantly, until it thickens, then pour it over the snails.

Consume the *escargots* at once, using spoons as utensils. (*Accompany them with a good supply of crusty French bread. Ed.*)

Foie gras de canard sauté aux céleris boules
DUCK LIVERS WITH CELERY ROOT

To serve 4:
- 1 pound duck livers (*see Note*)
- ½ pound celery root (*sometimes called celeriac; Ed.*)
- ½ lemon
- Salt
- 1 ounce truffles
- 4 tablespoons butter, in all
- 3 tablespoons ruby port
- 3 tablespoons juice from canned truffles, or cooking liquid if fresh truffles are used
- 1 cup Concentrated Veal Stock with Tomato (*demi-glace tomatée,* page 17)
- Coarse salt
- Freshly ground pepper

NOTE: *Duck livers can often be found sold in bulk in Chinese markets. If duck livers are unobtainable, substitute chicken livers. Ed.*

PREPARATION OF THE LIVERS:

The evening before preparing this dish, plunge the livers into a casserole of boiling salted water. Cook 1 minute, then let cool, and refrigerate them in the cooking liquid. This should be done in advance so that the livers will be firm.

NOTE: *Because our duck livers tend to be smaller in size and therefore cook more rapidly, remove the casserole from the heat as soon as the livers are added. After 3 minutes, add a few ice cubes to speed the cooling of the liquid. Also, if you have chicken stock at hand, it is preferable to water to use for cooking. This is because the livers of our ducks are not as flavorful as those found in France. Ed.*

The next day, take the livers from the cooking liquid and separate the two lobes. Remove any traces of green as well as filament. Using a sharp knife dipped into hot water, cut each piece of liver diagonally into slices about ½ inch thick. Arrange them on a plate and cover with aluminum foil. Keep cold until ready to use.

PREPARATION OF THE CELERY ROOT:

Peel the celery root thoroughly and wipe it with lemon to prevent darkening. Cut it into cubes and trim these approximately into the shape of an olive. Drop them into acidulated water until ready to cook.

Bring a large casserole of salted water to a boil and plunge in the celery root. Boil rapidly, uncovered, for about 6 minutes, keeping the balls firm; they are done when you can just crush one between two fingers. Drain the celery root and place under cold running water, then drain again.

PREPARATION OF THE SAUCE:

Cut the truffles into tiny dice. Melt 1 tablespoon of butter in a medium-size casserole and sauté the truffles 2 minutes over low heat. Deglaze the pan with port, and let it reduce until syrupy, then add the truffle juice and *demi-glace*. Bring the sauce to a simmer and cook 10 minutes over low heat. Skim the surface as needed.

At the last moment, stir in 2 tablespoons of butter, cut into small pieces. Taste for seasoning and add the celery root to warm gently.

FINISHING THE LIVER:

Over a low heat, melt the remaining 1 tablespoon butter *(add a little more if needed; Ed.)* in a skillet large enough to hold all the slices in one layer. Season the liver on both sides with salt and pepper and arrange in the pan. Cook 1 minute on each side, then divide the slices among 4 warm plates.

Return the sauce to a boil and spoon it over the liver. Scatter the *garniture* of celery root harmoniously over all and serve at once.

Huîtres chaudes aux bigorneaux
OYSTERS WITH PERIWINKLES
IN BUTTER SAUCE

(Color picture 2)

To serve 4:

    12 *belon* oysters (*see Note*)
    12 *Portugaise* oysters (*see Note*)
    144 periwinkles (*sea snails; see Note*)
    1 onion, thinly sliced
    2 carrots, thinly sliced
    1 stalk celery
    1 branch fresh thyme (*or substitute ½ teaspoon dried thyme; Ed.*)
    Coarse salt
    3 tablespoons distilled white vinegar
    ½ pound butter
    Freshly ground pepper, preferably white
    Juice of ½ lemon

NOTE: Belons *and* Portugaises *are two distinct varieties of oysters found in France. In the United States, depending where you live, choose two varieties of the freshest and tastiest oysters available. If you are limited to one kind of oyster, double the quantity.*

Periwinkles can frequently be found in Oriental markets, but if they are unavailable, the recipe can still succeed. In place of the court-bouillon *used to cook the periwinkles, substitute ½ cup of strained* court-bouillon, *page 20 or page 113, with the addition of 2 teaspoons vinegar.*

It is the spicy beurre fondu *with the vinegar accent that gives the recipe its character. Ed.*

HAVE READY:

1. The oysters: First open the *belons.* Hold them over a small casserole so as to catch their juice, detach them, and drop them into the casserole. Take care to keep any foreign matter from going in with them.

Do the same with the *Portugaises,* dropping them into a separate casserole.

Arrange half the empty shells (the deep halves) on two deep, heat-proof platters.

2. The periwinkles: Put the onion, carrot, celery, and thyme in a casserole with a good pinch of coarse salt, the vinegar, and 1 quart of water. Bring this *court-bouillon* to a boil and let simmer 15 minutes.

Wash the periwinkles, then plunge them into the casserole. Bring to a boil and skim the surface. Boil 3 minutes, then remove from heat.

Drain the periwinkles in a colander with a receptacle underneath to catch the *court-bouillon*. Then refresh them lightly with cold water to cool them just enough so that they can be handled.

With the help of a pin (or skewer), extract the periwinkles from their shells. Remove the black intestines and reserve the periwinkles in a bowl.

PREPARATION OF THE BUTTER:

Put ½ cup of the reserved *court-bouillon* in a small casserole and, over high heat, stir in the butter, cut into tiny pieces, using a wire whisk. The sauce should form a thick *liaison*. Taste for seasoning, adding pepper and lemon juice.

COOKING:

Warm the oysters in their separate casseroles. Bring them, at most, to 140° F. (This should take no longer than 2 minutes over medium heat.)

TO SERVE:

Preheat the broiler.

Warm the empty shells in the oven. When sufficiently heated, replace the oysters in the shells corresponding to each variety. Cover them with the sauce and distribute the periwinkles over all.

Put the oysters under the broiler for 20 seconds. Then divide 3 oysters of each variety among 4 plates and serve at once.

Quiche au sandre de Loire
QUICHE WITH FRESHWATER FISH

To serve 4:
  1 *sandre*, about 1¾ pounds (*see Note*)
  3 cups *court-bouillon* (page 20)
  Coarse salt
  Yeast Pastry Dough (*pâte à foncer fine*, page 31)
  4 eggs
  Salt
  Freshly ground pepper, preferably white
  3 tablespoons *crème fraîche* (page 22)
  Beurre fondu (page 81)

NOTE: *Sandre is a freshwater fish from the Loire River. It does not exist in the United States, but brook trout or other freshwater trout may be substituted successfully. Three fresh brook trout, weighing about 12 ounces each, will be sufficient. Poach them whole.*

Arrange the trout in cold court-bouillon *and bring the liquid slowly to a boil. When the water reaches a simmer, cover, remove the pan from heat, and let stand undisturbed, for 20 minutes. Then remove the skin and carefully bone the trout. Ed.*

HAVE READY:

1. The fish: After cleaning the *sandre*, cut the fillets off the bones and lay them, skin side down, in a shallow casserole. Cover the fish with *court-bouillon*, sprinkle with salt, and simmer over very low heat for 3 minutes.

Lift the fillets from the *court-bouillon*, drain, and let cool. Then remove the skin and break the fish into small pieces. Set aside on a plate.

2. The yeast pastry dough: Preheat oven to 425° F.

Sprinkle your work surface with a little flour and roll out the dough to form a circle 12 inches in diameter.

Lay a 10-inch pastry ring on a moistened baking sheet (*or use a tart mold with a detachable bottom; Ed.*), and center the dough over it. Turn the edges inward, forming double-thick sides, and cut off surplus dough by passing a rolling pin over the ring. Then heighten the sides by pinching them.

Prick the bottom of the pastry with a fork, cover it with a circle of wax paper, and weigh it down with a layer of dried beans (or rice). Bake the pastry shell for 10 to 15 minutes. Turn off the oven, remove the wax paper and dried beans, then let the shell dry in the oven for 10 minutes.

3. The filling: Break the eggs into a mixing bowl. Add salt, pepper, and *crème fraîche*. Mix thoroughly with a wire whisk, then pass the mixture through a fine sieve into another bowl.

COOKING THE QUICHE:

Reheat oven to 425° F.

Arrange the fish in the pastry shell. Rest it on its baking sheet on the oven rack, and carefully pour in the filling.

Lower heat to 375° F. and bake the quiche about 25 minutes. Remove from the oven and let stand 5 minutes.

TO SERVE:

Slide the quiche onto a round serving platter and remove the pastry ring. Serve the quiche accompanied by the *beurre fondu*.

Ragoût de truffes en chaussons
RAGOÛT OF TRUFFLES IN PASTRY SHELLS

NOTE: *At this writing, the quantity of truffles needed to prepare this recipe would cost approximately $70 (about $10 per ounce). I found that the recipe could also be prepared substituting 2 to 3 ounces imported dried mushrooms—such as* cèpes *or* morilles—*or 7 ounces of the most interesting fresh mushrooms available. In this case, replace the truffle juice with* demi-glace *(page 17) and, if you wish, add a modest quantity of truffles, cut into* julienne *strips. Ed.*

To serve 4:
    ½ pound Puff Pastry (*pâte feuilletée*, page 32)
    1 egg
    7 ounces truffles, fresh or preserved

2 tablespoons butter
1 shallot, finely chopped
Salt
Freshly ground pepper, preferably white
1½ tablespoons cognac
⅜ cup truffle juice
1 cup heavy cream
1 tablespoon *foie gras*

PREPARATION OF THE PASTRY SHELLS:

Preheat oven to 425° F.

The puff paste should have had all 6 turns and a good rest in the refrigerator. Roll it out into a band about ¼ inch thick and, using a circular cutting tool—such as an inverted glass or teacup—cut 4 circles, 4 inches in diameter. Then cut the circles in half to obtain 8 semi-circles. Lay them on a baking sheet that has been moistened lightly with cold water, and refrigerate 15 minutes.

Beat together the egg and 1 teaspoon of water in a small bowl, and brush the pastries with this. (Be careful not to brush the sides as this will cause them to rise unevenly.) With the point of a knife, draw an imprint, following the shape of each semicircle, about ¼ inch in from the edge; do not cut completely through the dough. Then, scratch a design of your choice on the lids of the pastries, barely penetrating the surface.

Bake the pastries 15 minutes. They should puff considerably. Keep them in a warm place until ready to serve.

PREPARATION OF THE TRUFFLES:

If the truffles are fresh, first cook them according to directions page 88, paragraph 2. Cut the truffles into matchstick *julienne*, each piece weighing roughly ⅙ ounce.

Melt the butter in a small casserole over low heat. Add the shallots and cook, covered, until soft, but not browned.

Add the truffles to the casserole, season with salt and pepper, and cook, covered, 2 minutes. Then deglaze the casserole with cognac, add truffle juice, and bring to a boil. Add the cream and cook over low heat until reduced by half. You should obtain a lightly thickened sauce. (*Allow about ½ hour for this, stirring frequently. Ed.*)

Just before serving, press the *foie gras* through a fine sieve and stir it into the sauce. Taste for seasoning.

TO SERVE:

With the point of a small knife, carefully pry open the shells, following their imprint. Reserve the lids. The shells should resemble elves' slippers. Place them in pairs on 4 hot plates, then divide the *ragoût* evenly among them. It should overflow slightly. Replace the lids and serve immediately.

Saumon et Saint-Pierre crus au sel de morue
MARINATED RAW FISH

To serve 4:
6-ounce fillet of very fresh salmon
6-ounce fillet of very fresh *Saint-Pierre* (*see Note*)
2 ounces dry salt cod
1 lemon
32 white peppercorns
32 coriander seeds
16 fresh tarragon leaves, coarsely chopped (*see Note*)
1 branch of parsley
½ cup imported virgin olive oil

NOTE: Saint-Pierre, *also called John Dory, is unavailable in this country, but fresh striped bass makes a perfect substitute.*

In case fresh tarragon is unavailable, do not use dried. However, you might try substituting a tablespoon of capers. Their color and taste work nicely with the raw fish. Ed.

PREPARATION OF THE FISH:

Have 4 well-chilled plates ready to receive the fish.

Using a long, sharp, flexible knife, slice the fillets on the diagonal, making the slices as wide and as thin as possible. Be certain that no skin, fatty film, or other matter remains.

Lay the slices on the cold plates, alternating their colors. Create an undulating pattern pleasing to the eye.

SEASONING THE FISH:

When purchasing the salt cod, choose a small piece that is very, very dry. Grate it to a powder on a cheese grater and further refine it by passing the powder through a sieve. Sprinkle this salty powder evenly over the slices of fish.

NOTE: *I recommend that you taste the powder before using it. Depending on the cod, it may not be salty enough to achieve the desired effect and simply taste like plain powdered fish. In this case, it might be better just to substitute a little coarse salt, preferably sea salt. Ed.*

Cover the entire surface of the fish with lemon juice, distributing it by tilting the plates back and forth.

Scatter 8 peppercorns and 8 coriander seeds over each plate and sprinkle with tarragon leaves. Create decorative divisions between the salmon and *Saint-Pierre* by slipping tiny sprigs of parsley between the slices.

Refrigerate the fish 15 minutes.

TO SERVE:

Hold each plate at a slight angle and let a few tablespoons of olive oil run slowly over the fish until the slices are coated entirely.

Serve the cold fish immediately, accompanied by large slices of toasted *pain de campagne*. (Pain de campagne *is a rough, round loaf of coarse-textured French or Italian bread. Ed.*)

Soufflé aux truffes
TRUFFLE SOUFFLÉ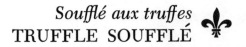

To serve 4:
    6 tablespoons butter, in all
    4 tablespoons flour
    1 cup milk
    ⅜ cup truffle juice
    Salt
    Freshly ground pepper, preferably white

5 ounces truffles, fresh or canned

4 eggs, separated

HAVE READY:

1. The sauce base: Melt 4 tablespoons of the butter in a small casserole over low heat. Add the flour and cook 3 minutes, stirring constantly with a wire whisk. Do not allow the *roux* to color.

Then add the milk, a little at a time, followed by the truffle juice. Mix vigorously, making sure that there are no lumps, and sprinkle lightly with salt. Reduce heat to as low as possible and cook 20 minutes. Stir frequently and make sure that the sauce remains below a simmer.

When the sauce has finished cooking, pass it through a fine sieve, then give it a brisk beating with a wire whisk. Keep the sauce warm in a double boiler (*bain-marie*).

2. The truffles: If they are fresh, cook them, tightly covered, for 20 minutes with 1 tablespoon cognac, 2 tablespoons dry white wine, ¾ cup water, salt, and pepper. Let them cool in the liquid, then proceed.

Using a *mandoline*, or other slicing device, cut 4 beautiful thin truffle slices and set them aside.

Cut 4 ounces of the truffles into a tiny dice and add them to the sauce. Finely chop the remaining pieces of truffle to use when preparing the molds.

3. The molds: Use the remaining 2 tablespoons of butter to grease liberally 4 ramekins or individual soufflé dishes. Then scatter the remaining chopped truffle evenly among them. (*If you think it necessary, attach a wax-paper collar to each mold. Ed.*)

4. The egg whites: Place the whites in a copper bowl and, using a wire whisk (*or electric mixer; Ed.*), beat them to a froth. Add a pinch of salt, and continue to beat until they are firm and can be held in a block upside down in the bowl.

PREPARATION AND COOKING OF THE SOUFFLÉ:

Preheat oven to 425° F.

When the whites are ready, incorporate the egg yolks into the hot sauce, stirring briskly. Then add one-quarter of the whites and stir until blended. This initial mixture will facilitate the incorporation of the rest of the whites. Add them all at once and, using a wooden spatula, fold them into the sauce.

Fill the prepared molds to four-fifths of their depth with the soufflé preparation, then arrange them on a baking sheet and place in the oven. Let them wait on the oven rack for 1 minute before closing the oven door. This will help the soufflé to rise.

The baking time should be no longer than about 10 minutes. Check them at this time, then let the soufflés remain inside the turned-off oven for 5 minutes.

Quickly decorate each soufflé with the reserved slices of truffle and serve immediately.

Tarte à la fourme du Cantal
CHEESE AND TOMATO TART

To serve 4 to 8:
    6 ounces Puff Pastry (*pâte feuilletée*, page 32)
    3 large, round tomatoes (*see Note*)
    Salt
    Freshly ground pepper
    3 tablespoons olive oil
    ½ pound *Cantal* cheese (*see Note*)
    1 rounded tablespoon tarragon mustard

NOTE: Cantal *is not a remarkable cheese, nor is it easy to find. However, substitutions are simple and economical. Danish* fontina *works perfectly, but Italian* fontina, *or* gouda *or* edam, *will also do very well. Ed.*

HAVE READY:

1. The pastry shell: Roll the cold pastry into a circle 12 inches in diameter. Lay it over a 10-inch tart ring placed on a moistened baking sheet (*or use a 10-inch tart form with a detachable bottom; Ed.*). Pass the rolling pin over it once to cut off excess dough. Pinch the edges of the pastry with thumb and index finger to make them protrude. They must then be folded inward to keep them from sticking to the ring so it can be removed after baking. Prick the bottom of the tart shell all over with the tines of a fork or point of a knife.

Chill the pastry 20 minutes, or longer, then preheat oven to 425° F.

Line the tart shell with a circle of wax paper, weigh it down with dried beans (or rice), and prebake it 12 to 15 minutes. Remove the wax paper and beans, and let the pastry cool slightly.

Lower oven temperature to 350° F.

2. The tomatoes: (*If tasty summer tomatoes are not in season, substitute 9 fresh Italian plum tomatoes. Ed.*)

Cut the tomatoes into thick slices, discarding the top and bottom pieces. Taking care not to damage the slices, poke out the water and seeds. Arrange the tomatoes on a plate, season well with salt and pepper, and baste with olive oil. Let marinate 15 minutes, turning them 2 or 3 times.

3. The cheese: Remove the rind and cut the cheese into thin slices.

Smear the mustard over the bottom of the tart shell, then cover it with approximately 2 layers of cheese slices.

FINISHING THE TART:

Arrange the tomatoes neatly over the cheese, then brush with their marinade.

Bake the tart 30 minutes, turn off the oven, and let it remain inside 20 minutes longer.

Remove the pastry ring and slide the tart onto a round serving platter.

This tart is best consumed hot, just as it comes from the oven. However, it may wait 15 minutes if necessary and be served warm.

Terrine de légumes "Olympe"
VEGETABLE TERRINE
(Color picture 15)

To serve 4:

    8 ounces young string beans

    10 ounces shelled fresh peas or, out of season, frozen peas may be used

    10 ounces small new carrots, peeled

6 medium-size to large artichokes
½ lemon
1 tablespoon butter
Salt

FILLING:

1 pound *jambon demi-sel* (*substitute Viriginia ham; Ed.*)
Juice of 2 lemons
½ teaspoon salt
¼ teaspoon freshly ground pepper
2 egg whites
1 cup imported French peanut oil

8 vine leaves, or if unavailable, substitute 4 lemons (*see Note*)
Uncooked Tomato Sauce (page 27)

NOTE: *Bottled vine leaves are readily available in Near Eastern stores, gourmet shops, and even many supermarkets. I find them preferable to lemon slices for holding the* terrine *together. Ed.*

PREPARE THE VEGETABLES:

1. Cook the string beans and peas separately in large amounts of boiling salted water. Allow 5 minutes for the beans and ½ minute for the peas. (*Be sure to keep them slightly undercooked as they will be cooked again. Ed.*) Drain, and refresh them in a basin of ice water. When they are chilled, drain again, and place in the refrigerator.

2. Cook the carrots whole, for 8 minutes, in the same manner.

3. Trim the tops and bottoms of the artichokes and wipe with lemon to prevent them from darkening. Melt 1 tablespoon of butter in a casserole large enough to hold them side by side. Add the artichokes, cover the casserole, and cook over low heat for 10 minutes to bring out their flavor.

Then add salt and add enough water to cover the artichokes completely. To protect their color, cover them with a sheet of wax paper cut to fit the shape of the casserole. Re-cover the casserole, bring the water to a simmer, and cook slowly for 20 to 30 minutes, depending on their size.

Let the artichokes cool in the liquid, then drain. Remove all the leaves and the chokes, and trim the bottoms so that they are smooth and even. Chill thoroughly in the refrigerator.

PREPARATION OF THE FILLING (*la farce*):

It is important that the blender or food-processor container be ice-cold. We recommend placing it in the freezer or chilling it with ice for some time before it is to be used.

While the container is chilling, remove any sinews, fat, or gristle from the ham, and cut the meat into a tiny dice. Place the ham, also, in the freezer or a very cold place for a minimum of 30 minutes.

NOTE: *If one is using a blender, the ingredients of the filling may have to be divided in half and prepared in two batches; or the ham may be ground alone in several stages before the oil is added. Be sure the first portion is returned to the refrigerator to keep cold and that the blender container is chilled again before preparing the next portion. Ed.*

Take the chilled container from the freezer and put in the ham, lemon juice, and seasonings; blend briefly, then add the egg whites. When the whites are well blended, incorporate the oil a little at a time. Though the oil has to be added slowly, the whole operation should be completed as quickly as possible so that the filling does not become warm. If necessary, return the blender container to the freezer.

PREPARATION OF THE *terrine*:

Preheat oven to 325° F.

Choose a nonmetallic, rectangular mold 9 inches by 5 inches and 2½ to 3 inches deep. Drape the bottom and sides of the mold with vine leaves. (*Rinse and drain them well before using. Ed.*) Or if they are unavailable, line the *terrine* with thin slices of lemon, peeled close to the flesh. All the vegetables must be very cold and completely dry. Reserve a few string beans for decoration later when serving the *terrine*.

The construction: Spread a thin bed of ham filling over the bottom of the *terrine* and arrange neat rows of carrots over it. Add another layer of filling, then the string beans, packed together tightly in one layer.

Spread more filling over the beans, then arrange the artichoke bottoms, cut in half so as to fit together as closely as possible. Add more filling, followed by the peas in an even layer.

Finish with the remainder of the filling. Fold the vine leaves over the top of the *terrine* and cover it with a sheet of buttered wax paper.

Set the *terrine* in a pan of boiling water and bake for 30 minutes.

Cool the *terrine* in the pan of water and chill at least 8 hours, or preferably overnight, before unmolding.

Pour a ladle of tomato sauce onto each of 4 cold plates. Carefully cut the *terrine* into slices ¾ inch thick and arrange them over the sauce. (*When you slice the* terrine, *have a large spatula handy to catch each slice in one piece and facilitate its transfer to the serving plate. Ed.*) Add a *garniture* of a few extra string beans, scattered at random, and serve at once.

Tourte de pommes de terre
VEAL AND POTATO PIE

This is an adaptation of an old *bourbonnaise* recipe called *pâté au tartouffe.*

To serve 4:
   2 large Idaho potatoes, about ¾ pound in all
   6 ounces boneless fillet of veal
   Coarse salt
   Freshly ground pepper
   2 large shallots, chopped
   1½ tablespoons butter
   1 pound Puff Pastry (*pâte feuilletée*, page 32)
   2 tablespoons chopped chives
   2 tablespoons chopped fresh chervil or parsley
   1 egg
   ⅔ cup *crème fraîche* (page 22)

HAVE READY:

1. Peel and rinse the potatoes. Cut them in thin, even slices with the help of a *mandoline* or other slicing device, then cover with ice water until ready to use.

2. Remove all sinews from the veal, and cut the meat into long thin strips. Sprinkle with salt and pepper.

3. Sauté the shallots in butter, covered, for 2 minutes over low heat. Set aside.

4. Divide the puff pastry into two pieces. On a floured marble surface, or worktable, roll out two circles of dough, one larger than the other—8 inches and 10 inches in diameter respectively.

Moisten a baking sheet with cold water and lay the smaller circle of dough over it. Place the larger circle between two sheets of wax paper and rest it on top of the other. Refrigerate the pastry until ready to proceed.

PREPARATION OF THE *tourte*:

Preheat oven to 425° F.

Drain the potatoes, and dry them in a towel. Mix well with salt and pepper, then add the chives and chervil, and continue mixing until the herbs are evenly distributed. Add the sautéed shallot and strips of veal to the potatoes, again making sure that everything is evenly distributed.

Working quickly, take the pastry from the refrigerator, remove the larger circle, and set it aside. Arrange the potato and veal mixture in a mound in the center of the smaller circle, leaving an outside border of 2 inches.

Moisten the border with cold water, then lay the larger circle of dough on top. Carefully bring up the edges of the bottom circle, turning the top and bottom edges one into the other and rolling them to seal in the filling completely.

Beat together the egg and a teaspoon of cold water in a small bowl. Using a brush, paint the entire surface of the *tourte* with the egg. Using the back of a knife, draw a circle 5 inches in diameter around the top of the *tourte*. (*Do not cut through the dough!*) Decorate the rest of the pastry to your own taste.

BAKING THE *tourte*:

Place the *tourte* in the oven and bake 30 minutes. Meanwhile, heat the *crème fraîche* in a small saucepan.

Take the *tourte* from the oven and detach the lid, cutting through the 5-inch circle with the point of a knife. Pour boiling *crème fraîche* into the opening, while simultaneously lifting the filling slightly with a fork to distribute the cream within. Replace the lid and return the *tourte* to the oven for 15 minutes.

When finished, remove from the oven and let the *tourte* stand at room temperature for 15 minutes before serving.

TO SERVE:

Slip a metal spatula under the pastry to loosen it and slide the *tourte* from the baking sheet onto a round platter covered with a paper doily. Use a wide, sharp knife to serve.

Accompany this dish with a simple *beurre fondu,* page 160, paragraph 2, or a green salad prepared with a walnut-oil dressing.

Les poissons, crustacés & coquillages

FISH & SHELLFISH

Coquilles Saint-Jacques à la vapeur

STEAMED SCALLOPS WITH AROMATIC VEGETABLES

To serve 4:

    8½ pounds live sea scallops (*1½ pounds shucked; Ed.*)

    10 tablespoons butter, in all

    Salt

    Freshly ground pepper

    4 large cooking-spoonfuls of aromatic vegetables (*see Note*) from
        court-bouillon (page 20)

    ½ cup dry white wine

    ½ lemon

    2 tablespoons coarsely chopped parsley, preferably flat-leafed

PREPARATION OF THE SCALLOPS:

If the scallops have not already been shucked (*the way they are usually sold in the United States; Ed.*), open them at the last moment in the following manner:

Slip the blade of a short, sturdy knife between the two shells and cut the muscle that retains them. Using a spoon, carefully detach the meat fixed to the concave part of the shell.

Separate the white meat, then the coral (*in the United States, fish merchants do not retain the coral as they do in Europe; Ed.*), and

1 Broiled Tomatoes Stuffed with Egg and Spinach

2 Oysters with Periwinkles in Butter Sauce

3 Pheasant Salad

4 *Salmon Scallops with Sorrel Sauce*

5 Red Mullet with Beef Marrow

6 Sole with Chives

7 *Pigeon with Garlic Sauce*

8 1 *Petits Fours*

2 *Mille-feuilles*

3 *Three-layer Chocolate Cake with Candied Grapefruit Peel*

4 *Peaches and Almonds in Red Wine*

5 *Fruit Goblet*

6 *Apple Tart*

7 *Kiwi Custard Tart*

8 *Floating Island*

9 *Poached and Fresh Fruits with
Ices and Raspberry Sauce*

9 *Molded Ham Crêpes*

*10 Three-layer Chocolate Cake with
Candied Grapefruit Peel*

11 Five Courses from One Kettle

12 *Chestnut Soufflé*   *Saddle of Venison with White Peppercorns*

13 Filet Mignon with Shallots

14 Duck with Black Currants

15 Vegetable Terrine

wash them in several changes of water to remove all traces of sand. Split the white meat in half, through the thickest part, cutting *with* the grain.

Place a stainless-steel vegetable-steamer rack inside a medium-size casserole (or use a *couscoussière*). Butter the rack liberally and arrange the scallops (and roes, if any) on it. Sprinkle them with salt and pepper and add the cooked vegetable *garniture* taken from the *court-bouillon*. Dot the scallops lavishly with the remaining butter and pour the wine over them.

NOTE: *If you have prepared a* court-bouillon *before and, perhaps, strained and reserved the remaining broth (it freezes well), it may be reused here. Heat the* court-bouillon, *adding one-third the quantities given for carrots, celery, onion, and shallots in the original recipe. Boil 4 minutes, and spoon this fresh* garniture *over the scallops. Ed.*

COOKING:

Cover the casserole and place it over high heat. At the first sign of a simmer from the wine below, remove from the heat and let stand, covered, for 5 minutes.

Uncover the casserole and return it to the stove. Boil 1 minute, allowing the butter that has melted from above to form a *liaison* with the liquid below. Sprinkle the scallops with a squeeze of lemon juice and scatter the parsley over all.

Remove the rack from the casserole and serve the scallops and their vegetable garniture in deep plates. Moisten with sauce from the bottom of the casserole and, if you wish, pass more of it separately.

Escalopes de saumon à l'oseille Troisgros
SALMON SCALLOPS WITH SORREL SAUCE

(Color picture 4)

To serve 4:
    2 pounds fresh salmon
    4 ounces fresh sorrel leaves, about 1 quart tightly packed
    1 quart Fish Stock (*fumet de poisson,* page 20)
    ⅓ cup Sancerre, or other dry white wine

3 tablespoons dry vermouth
2 shallots, chopped
1⅔ cups *crème fraîche* (page 22)
3 tablespoons butter
½ lemon
Coarse salt
Freshly ground pepper, preferably white
1 to 2 tablespoons imported peanut oil

HAVE READY:

1. The salmon: Choose a piece of salmon from the thickest center section of the fish. Using a flexible boning knife, cut apart the two fillets and carefully remove the skin.

With pliers, pull out the tiny bones hiding in the center of the flesh. You will find them by running your fingers against the grain of the fish.

Divide the fillets in two lengthwise, making 4 pieces weighing about 6 ounces each.

Slip the salmon between two sheets of lightly oiled wax paper and, with a wooden mallet (*or the flat side of a meat cleaver; Ed.*), flatten it slightly to scallops of equal thicknesses.

2. The sorrel: Remove the stems and strip off the central vein of the leaves, working from bottom to top. Wash the sorrel and tear the larger leaves into 2 or 3 pieces.

PREPARATION OF THE SAUCE:

Put the fish stock, wine, vermouth, and shallots together in a large heavy saucepan or casserole and, over high heat, boil down the liquid until it is bright and syrupy and reduced nearly to a glaze.

Add the *crème fraîche* and boil until the sauce becomes slightly thickened.

Drop the sorrel into the sauce and cook together for just 25 seconds, then remove from the heat. Swirling the casserole, or stirring with a wooden spoon (do not use a whisk, as it will catch on the sorrel leaves), incorporate the butter, cut into tiny pieces. Complete the seasoning with a few drops of lemon juice and salt and pepper.

TO COOK THE SALMON:

Warm a large skillet, adding just barely enough oil to coat the bottom. If you use a "nonstick" pan, no oil is needed.

On their less presentable side, season the salmon scallops with salt and pepper, then place them in the skillet, seasoned side up. Cook 25 seconds, then turn carefully to the second side and cook 15 seconds longer. The salmon must be undercooked to preserve its tenderness (*and it will continue to cook in the finished hot sauce; Ed.*).

TO SERVE:

Distribute the hot sorrel sauce in the centers of 4 large heated plates and, after having first sponged off any excess oil with a paper towel, place the salmon scallops, seasoned side down, on the sauce. Sprinkle lightly with coarse salt.

This dish suffers if it must wait and should be prepared at the last moment.

Feuillée de morue Berchoux
COD MOUSSE WITH BAKED POTATOES

NOTE: *The Troisgros have treated this recipe as a humble dish to be accompanied only by hot baked potatoes. And, while it is indeed simple, it invites embellishment. If you choose, the* morue *(with the potatoes) may also be accompanied by fried croûtons, hard-cooked eggs, hot cooked carrots, string beans, and (in season) artichokes. All are harmonious with the salt cod and, when colorfully presented together, give the* morue *the same garlicky and visual festivity of a dish such as a Provençal* aïoli. *Ed.*

To serve 6:
>   1½ pounds salt cod
>   *Bouquet garni* (sprigs of thyme and parsley and a bay leaf, tied together)
>   Juice of ½ lemon
>   2 cloves garlic, finely chopped
>   4 anchovy fillets, cut into tiny pieces
>   Freshly ground white pepper
>   ⅝ cup olive oil
>   Heavy cream, about ⅔ cup (*optional*)
>   1¾ ounces truffles, thinly sliced (optional)
>   6 hot baked potatoes

PREPARATION OF THE SALT COD (*la morue*):

Choose the cod as white as possible and from the most recent catch.

Place it skin side up on a rack in a large basin of cold water. Soak the cod for 48 hours, changing the water 3 or 4 times.

No more than 2 hours before serving time, drain the cod, cut it into 4 manageable pieces and, using scissors, cut off the fins.

Put the fish into a large casserole with 2 to 3 quarts of cold water and the *bouquet garni*. Over medium heat, bring the water slowly to a boil, uncovered, and as soon as a simmer is reached, reduce the heat so that no bubbles are apparent on the surface of the water. Cook the cod 20 minutes from this moment. Then, remove from heat and let the cod cool slightly, or just long enough so that it can be handled. Drain in a colander. (*The cod must be warm when it is blended with the other ingredients. Ed.*)

FINISHING THE MOUSSE:

Remove all skin and bones from the fish, and flake the meat with your fingers. (*This will also help you to find any bones that may have escaped your attention. Ed.*)

In a saucepan, bring ⅓ cup of water to a boil. Off heat, add the flaked cod, lemon juice, garlic, anchovies, and a generous amount of pepper.

At the same time, in two small saucepans, warm the oil over low heat until almost smoking and bring the cream to a simmer.

Stirring vigorously without stopping (*I suggest using an electric mixer for this procedure; Ed.*), beat the oil into the fish, a little at a time. It will help to rest the pan within a larger pan of very hot water (a *bain-marie*). However, the temperature of the mixture should not go above 145° F.

The cod and the oil should form a *liaison*, making a thick paste. Taste for seasoning; you may wish to add more pepper. (*At this point, if you are not satisfied with the texture, also beat in the hot cream, a little at a time. This will help to create a more creamy liaison. Ed.*)

TO SERVE:

Mound the salt-cod mousse in the center of a warm serving platter, and surround it with hot baked potatoes. You may enrich the presentation by garnishing the mousse with slices of truffle first dipped in olive oil.

Filets de rouget à la moelle de boeuf
RED MULLET WITH BEEF MARROW

(Color picture 5)

To serve 4:

4 ounces beef marrow
6 red mullet, about 7 ounces each (*see Note*)
Salt
Freshly ground pepper
Flour
3 tablespoons peanut oil
6 tablespoons butter, in all
3 large shallots, chopped
1 cup dry red Burgundy
2 rounded tablespoons Fresh Tomato Sauce (*coulis de tomates,*
   page 23)
Powdered salt cod (page 87), or sea salt

NOTE: *Red mullet is most plentiful in the Southern part of the United States. If it is not obtainable in your region, try substituting 2 small red snappers, about 1 pound each. They will have the same colorful appearance as red mullet and an excellent, though different, flavor. Ed.*

HAVE READY:

1. The marrow: The day before preparing this dish, have your butcher extract 2 firm cylinders of marrow from beef bones. Soak them for 12 hours in ice water. Then drain and slice into rounds ½ inch thick.

2. The fish: Clean the red mullet (*or snapper*) and, using a flexible fillet knife, remove the fillets from the central bone. Dry them with paper towels and sprinkle with salt and pepper. Dredge the fillets in flour, tapping them lightly to remove any excess.

COOKING:

In an oval sauté pan (*poêle à poisson*), heat the oil with 2 tablespoons of butter. When it foams, arrange the fillets, skin side down, in the pan and cook 2 minutes on each side. Shake the pan occasionally to make sure that the fillets do not stick.

Meanwhile, put the marrow in a small saucepan and cover it with 2 cups of cold salted water. Place the pan over medium heat, and at the first sign of a simmer, remove it from the stove. Drain well just before using.

PREPARATION OF THE SAUCE:

Place the fish on a hot serving platter, skin side up, and cover it to keep warm.

In the sauté pan, add the shallots to the remaining butter and oil. Cook, covered, 2 minutes over low heat to release their juices.

Deglaze the pan with red wine, add the tomato sauce, and reduce until only ½ cup of sauce remains. Remove the pan from the heat and, using a small wire whisk, stir in the remaining 4 tablespoons of butter, cut into tiny pieces. Taste for seasoning and be generous with freshly ground pepper.

TO SERVE:

Coat the fillets with sauce and place the slices of drained hot marrow on top. Sprinkle the marrow with a pinch of powdered salt cod, or sea salt, and serve at once.

Gigot de mer braisé aux nouilles fraîches
BRAISED FISH WITH FRESH NOODLES

To serve 4:
> 1 whole goosefish (*monkfish or "bellyfish"; see Note*), weighing about 1¾ pounds without the head
> 3 cloves garlic, peeled
> Coarse salt
> Freshly ground pepper
> 5 tomatoes
> 3 tablespoons butter
> 1 carrot, sliced
> 1 onion, quartered
> *Bouquet garni* (sprigs of thyme and parsley and a bay leaf, tied together)
> ½ cup dry white wine

½ cup *crème fraîche* (page 22)
1 teaspoon (⅙ ounce) saffron threads
6 ounces fresh noodles (see page 212)

NOTE: *The French call this fish* lotte *and it can be found in the western Atlantic from the Grand Banks to North Carolina. It is large and thick-fleshed, has a central bone, and sports a huge, notoriously ugly head. Only the tail section is saved for eating.*

Large retail fish markets that also cater to the restaurant trade sometimes carry it and it is sold under a variety of names. But, because it is not easily obtained, I have translated this recipe with an alternate, and shorter, cooking time. The alternate timing is applicable to most firm-fleshed fish that you might wish to substitute. Excellent choices would be young cod, striped bass, halibut, and pollack. Ed.

HAVE READY:

1. The fish: Remove the skin and the fins. With a small sharp knife, make 6 notches, at regular intervals, on both sides of the fish. Split the cloves of garlic in half lengthwise, and insert one in each notch. Season well with salt and pepper and set aside.

2. The tomatoes: Drop the tomatoes into boiling water. Count to 10, remove, and plunge them into cold water. When they have cooled, peel them, cut in half, and squeeze out the seeds and excess water. Cut the tomatoes into small dice.

COOKING THE FISH:

Melt the butter in an oval casserole large enough to hold the entire fish, and brown the goosefish on both sides over high heat. (*Turn the fish carefully, using two spatulas. Ed.*) Allow about 5 minutes for each side. (*Two minutes should be sufficient for most other fish. Ed.*)

Surround the fish with the carrot, onion, and *bouquet garni*, and cover the casserole tightly. Barely simmer the goosefish for 20 minutes over low heat (*5 minutes for most fish; Ed.*), then moisten with white wine. Cook, covered, 25 minutes, basting several times (*10 minutes or less, for most other fish; Ed.*).

PREPARATION OF THE SAUCE:

Uncover the fish, add the *crème fraîche*, and bring the cooking liquid to a boil. At the first sign of a simmer, carefully remove the fish, and place it on a hot platter. Cover to keep warm.

Pass the sauce through a fine sieve or food mill (*see Note*) into a medium-size saucepan and add the saffron and diced tomato. Boil gently until reduced and slightly thickened. Taste for seasoning.

NOTE: *If you are following the shorter cooking schedule, you might prefer to leave the vegetables whole. They will be perfectly cooked, whereas, given the longer cooking time, they should be puréed. Ed.*

COOKING THE NOODLES:

Drop the noodles into a large kettle of boiling salted water. Cook until *al dente*, done but firm to the tooth. Seven to 8 minutes should be sufficient, but check them after 5 minutes, as the thicknesses of fresh noodles vary. When they are ready, add ½ cup of cold water to stop their cooking, and drain well in a colander.

FINISHING THE FISH:

Preheat oven to 450° F.

Arrange the hot drained noodles around the bottom of a long deep platter. Place the fish in the center and rewarm the dish for 30 seconds in the oven. Then, pour boiling sauce over all and serve at once. The flesh of the fish should separate easily from the central bone.

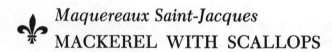

Maquereaux Saint-Jacques
MACKEREL WITH SCALLOPS

To serve 4:
    4 fresh striped mackerel, whole (*see Note*)
    Salt
    Freshly ground pepper
    8 sea scallops
    4 tablespoons butter, in all
    1 small carrot, minced
    2 shallots, minced
    1 clove garlic, minced
    2 tomatoes, chopped

32 coriander seeds
½ cup dry white wine
Juice of ½ lemon
1 tablespoon chopped parsley

HAVE READY:

1. The mackerel: The mackerel must be very fresh with bright rose gills. After choosing the youngest, clean them, cut off the fins, and wash well under running water.

Using a fillet knife, cut along the backbone from the inside, detaching the flesh from it. Cut the backbone at both ends with scissors and pull it out.

NOTE: *This dish can also be made with mackerel fillets, the pairs of fillets held together with round toothpicks. Ed.*

At regular intervals, make 4 diagonal slashes along three-quarters of the length of each mackerel on one side. Season with salt and pepper and set aside.

2. The scallops: If live scallops are used, clean them as described in the recipe for Steamed Scallops with Aromatic Vegetables (*coquilles Saint-Jacques à la vapeur*, page 96).

Divide the scallops in half, through the thickest part, cutting *with* the grain. Season with salt and pepper and tuck half a scallop securely into each of the incisions made along the surface of the mackerel. They will protrude slightly above the fish.

COOKING:

Preheat oven to 450° F.

Over low heat, melt 1½ tablespoons of butter in a baking dish, large enough to hold the mackerel side by side. Distribute the vegetable *garniture* and the coriander seeds evenly over the bottom of the dish. Cook the *garniture*, covered, for 2 minutes to release the juices of the vegetables, then arrange the fish on top.

Moisten the mackerel with white wine and lemon juice, then cut the remaining butter into small pieces and scatter it over all. Cover the fish with a piece of wax paper cut to fit the baking dish.

Bring the liquid to a simmer over moderate heat, then place the mackerel in the hot oven for 18 minutes.

TO SERVE:

Carefully arrange the mackerel on a heated serving platter and spoon the *garniture* over them.

At this time, the broth remaining in the baking dish should be syrupy enough to glaze the fish. If not, boil it down, either in the baking dish or a small saucepan, until it is reduced to ½ cup. Taste for seasoning and spoon the syrup over the fish.

Serve hot, sprinkled with chopped parsley.

Merlan "Hôtel des Platanes"
WHITING WITH MUSHROOMS

To serve 4:
    4 whiting, about 10 to 12 ounces each
    Salt
    Freshly ground pepper
    ¾ cup milk
    ½ pound firm white mushrooms
    8 tablespoons butter, in all
    2 medium-size onions, chopped
    Flour

HAVE READY:

1. The whiting: Choose 4 bright-eyed fish. Clean them, cutting off the fins and tails; then rinse, and wipe them dry with a towel. Using a sharp knife, make 1-inch slashes, barely penetrating the flesh, diagonally along both sides of each fish.

Season the whiting well with salt and pepper and soak them in milk. (*Soak them in the smallest dish possible—just large enough to hold the fish side by side. Ed.*) Turn them several times.

2. The mushrooms: Trim the stems and rinse briefly under running water. Do not give them a chance to soak. Dry well in a towel, then chop the mushrooms coarsely.

Melt 2 tablespoons of butter in a medium-size skillet, and sauté the onions until soft and golden, but not browned. Add the mushrooms and cook, stirring constantly, until all moisture has evaporated and the skillet is dry. Sprinkle with salt and pepper and set aside.

COOKING:

Preheat oven to 475° F.

Roll the whiting in flour, coating thoroughly.

Melt 4 tablespoons of butter in an oval pan large enough to hold the fish side by side. When the butter begins to brown, arrange the whiting in it. Cook 4 minutes on each side, then put them in the hot oven for another 4 to 5 minutes.

TO SERVE:

Carefully arrange the whiting on a hot serving platter. Add the remaining 2 tablespoons of butter to the cooking pan and heat it until the butter foams. Quickly add the mushroom-onion mixture and, stirring continuously, sauté over high heat until nicely browned.

Cover the whiting with the mushrooms and onions and serve at once. Time the service of your meal carefully as this dish cannot wait.

Navarin de homard

LOBSTER STEW WITH VEGETABLES

To serve 4:

    4 pounds live female lobster (*two 2-pound lobsters; see Note*)
    Salt
    Freshly ground pepper
    6 tablespoons butter, in all
    ⅜ cup olive oil
    2 shallots, minced
    1 carrot, minced
    2 tablespoons cognac
    ½ cup dry white wine
    1 cup Fish Stock (*fumet de poisson*, page 20)
    2 large fresh tomatoes, chopped (2 heaping cups)
    1 rounded teaspoon tomato paste
    Bouquet garni (sprigs of thyme and parsley and a bay leaf, tied
        together)
    ½ cup *crème fraîche* (page 22)

VEGETABLE *garniture*:

2 ounces (1 cup) string beans, cut in half
3 ounces (1 cup) shelled peas
About 1 pound new potatoes
2 carrots, about ½ pound
2 turnips, about ¾ pound
Coarse salt

NOTE: *The availability of lobster in the United States is still far greater than in France, where it is extremely scarce and expensive. After testing this recipe, my feeling was that the effort put forth in making such a delicious sauce would have been more rewarding if one found a larger portion of lobster meat among the vegetables of the* garniture. *It would not be amiss to use more, and smaller, lobsters. Ed.*

HAVE READY:

1. The vegetables: Cook the string beans and peas separately in large amounts of boiling salted water. Boil the string beans 6 minutes and the peas 1 minute. Drain, and plunge them into a basin of ice water. When they are chilled, drain again.

Cut the vegetables—potatoes, carrots, and turnips—into neat pieces of equal size, making about 16 pieces of each vegetable. Cook the vegetables separately in rapidly boiling salted water until just done, then drain, refresh them briefly in cold water, and drain again.

2. The lobsters: Choose lively female lobsters. (*They can be distinguished by the small "feelers" running along the tail. Female "feelers" have coarse hairy edges, while male "feelers" are smooth. Ed.*)

Hold each lobster securely on a chopping board and, using a large heavy knife, or meat cleaver, sever the tail from the body. Split the body in two lengthwise, and discard the small stomach pocket in the top of the head.

Remove the pale-green tomalley and dark-green roe. Put them together in a bowl.

Detach the claws and sprinkle all the pieces of the lobster with salt and pepper.

COOKING:

In a large heavy casserole, heat 1½ tablespoons of butter with the oil until smoking. Add the lobster pieces and cook them over high heat, turning on all sides until the shells become bright red.

Reduce the heat slightly and scatter the *mirepoix* of minced shallot and carrot over all. Moisten with cognac and, when the liquid evaporates, pour in the white wine, followed by the fish stock. Stir in the fresh tomato and the tomato paste, then add the *bouquet garni*. Bring the broth to a vigorous boil. Then lower the heat, maintaining a gentle simmer, and cook the lobster, uncovered, for 15 minutes. Turn frequently, spooning the sauce over the shells.

Using tongs, remove the lobster from the casserole. Set aside the tail and claw sections, and chop up the bodies into pieces as small as possible. (*The Troisgros would probably use a heavy-duty restaurant food processor to grind the shells. I do not believe that home kitchen equipment is up to this task unless the lobsters used are of a very small size. I found it necessary to use a meat cleaver, aided by a mallet, to break up the shells. Ed.*)

Return the shells and all the juices to the casserole. Boil them in the sauce gently for 10 minutes, turning frequently and pressing down on them with a wooden spoon.

In a small bowl, blend the remaining butter with the tomalley and roe. Add this *liaison* to the sauce, which will take on a bright vermilion cast. Pour in the *crème fraîche* and continue to cook the sauce for 3 minutes, stirring constantly. Taste for seasoning.

Using the fine blade of a food mill, over a clean casserole, squeeze out all the sauce and juices from the shattered shells. Do this operation in several stages, discarding the shells when every bit of lobster essence has been removed. Keep the sauce warm over very low heat.

FINISHING THE *navarin*:

Using poultry shears, cut through the underside of the tail shell and remove the meat in one piece, then slice it into round medallions. Snip the claws as necessary, and extract the meat. Cut it into even pieces.

Add the lobster meat to the sauce along with the cooked potatoes, carrots, and turnips. Warm them together without allowing the sauce to boil. As they reheat, turn them over carefully in the sauce.

At the last moment, reheat the string beans and peas by dropping them briefly into boiling salted water. Drain well.

Serve the *navarin* either from the casserole or from a heated serving tureen, with the string beans and peas scattered over it.

Panaché aux six poissons "Ajano"
POACHED MIXED FISH WITH A VEGETABLE GARNITURE

NOTE: *The idea of this dish is to have an attractive medley of fish with a variation of colors, but somewhat uniform thicknesses for even cooking. All the fish should be filleted, but the skin should be left intact. Possible exceptions might be fish such as halibut, sold in steaks, or sole, which is usually sold in skinless fillets.*

In France one would use rougets, loup, daurade, rascasse, vives, *and* barbue. *Excellent substitutes from our waters would be red mullet, striped bass, sea bass, whiting, flounder, and red snapper.*

Most important, the fish should be absolutely fresh, even if this means reducing the variety to three or four different fish rather than six. In this case, simply buy larger portions of the fish you choose. This recipe can be easily increased or reduced to serve a larger or smaller number of people. Ed.

To serve 6:

THE FISH:

(These are suggested weights before filleting. Have them all filleted at the market. Ed.)
   3 red mullet, about ½ pound each
   2 pounds striped bass
   1¾ pounds sea bass
   2 flounder, about 1½ pounds each
   3 whiting
   1¾ pounds red snapper

   3 carrots
   3 small turnips
   4 ounces string beans
   4 ounces fresh peas, about 2 ounces shelled (*substitute frozen if necessary; Ed.*)
   2 tomatoes
   Salt
   Freshly ground pepper
   16 tablespoons butter, in all

1 shallot, finely chopped
1 cup dry white wine
Juice of ½ lemon
1 tablespoon chopped parsley, preferably flat-leafed

HAVE READY:

1. Peel the carrots and turnips, cut into large dice, and trim these into neat balls or ovals. There should be about 30 pieces of each vegetable.

Trim the ends off the string beans and cut them into even lengths of about 1½ inches.

2. Drop the carrots, turnips, and string beans into separate saucepans of boiling salted water. Cook each, uncovered, for 5 minutes, then quickly drain in a colander, and plunge them into a basin of ice water. When the vegetables are chilled, drain them again, and set aside with the uncooked shelled peas.

3. Drop the tomatoes into boiling water, count to 10, remove, and plunge them into cold water. Peel, seed, and dice the tomatoes. Then season with salt and pepper.

4. Divide the fish fillets into portions that will assure each person a medallion of each variety. Sprinkle with salt and pepper.

COOKING:

Smear a very large shallow sauté pan with softened butter and scatter the shallot over the bottom.

Group the fish in the pan, keeping each variety together, and add the wine. Bring to a boil over moderate heat and baste the fish. Cover and reduce the heat to a simmer. Cook the fish from 5 to 10 minutes, or until just done. Check and baste the fish after the first 5 minutes.

With the help of a large spatula (to hold the fish in place), carefully pour all the liquid from the sauté pan into a heavy 1-quart saucepan. Cover the fish and set aside. (*At this time, ready a large saucepan of boiling salted water for reheating the vegetables. Ed.*)

Boil down the stock from the fish until reduced by half. Lower the heat and, using a wire whisk, beat in the butter, cut into tiny pieces. A slightly thickened, creamy *liaison* will be formed. Taste for seasoning and stir in the juice of half a lemon and the parsley.

TO SERVE:

Working quickly, arrange a portion of each fish on six hot plates, creating a star pattern, and nap with the hot butter sauce.

Drop the vegetables, except for the tomatoes, into a pan of boiling water, then drain immediately. (*Do not refresh them. Ed.*)

Strew the hot vegetables over and around the fish, adding the cold diced tomato last. Serve at once.

NOTE: *This dish is, also, extremely attractive with the fish arranged on a large hot platter presented at the table before serving. Ed.*

Raie bouclée à l'huile et au vinaigre
SKATE WITH OIL AND VINEGAR SAUCE

To serve 4:
    1 large skate wing, about 2 pounds (*see Note*)
    1 onion, thinly sliced
    1 carrot, thinly sliced
    2 teaspoons peppercorns, slightly crushed
Bouquet garni (sprigs of thyme and parsley and a bay leaf, tied
        together)
    ⅜ cup distilled white vinegar
    2 tablespoons coarse salt

    SAUCE:

    1 teaspoon table salt
    ½ teaspoon freshly ground pepper
    ⅓ cup wine vinegar
    ⅔ cup imported olive oil
    3 tablespoons coriander seeds
    1 shallot, finely chopped

Hot new potatoes, cooked in their jackets.
Whole parsley leaves (*preferably the small young leaves of flat-
        leafed parsley; Ed.*)

NOTE: *In the United States, the most edible variety of skate is the thornback. Avoid the sand skate. This method of preparation also works perfectly for trout and the timing is exactly the same. However, do not remove the skin from trout before cooking. Ed.*

PREPARE THE SKATE:

Remove the dark thorny skin and cut the wing into 4 equal portions parallel with the bones. Rinse them well and remove any viscosity found on the white skin.

COOKING:

Scatter the sliced onion and carrot over the bottom of a large casserole. Add the crushed peppercorns and *bouquet garni* and arrange the skate over the *garniture*. Add 1 quart of cold water, the distilled white vinegar, and coarse salt.

Bring the liquid slowly to a boil over moderate heat and, at the first sign of a simmer, cover the casserole and remove it from the stove. Let the fish stand undisturbed for 20 minutes.

THE SAUCE:

In a small bowl, mix together the table salt, ground pepper, and wine vinegar. Using a wire whisk, incorporate the oil a little at a time, then add the coriander and shallot. Set aside.

FINISHING THE SKATE:

Using a fork and a skimmer, carefully remove each piece of skate from the cooking liquid, and lay it on a baking sheet. With the help of a knife, pull off the remaining white skin and trim away any gelatinous areas. When each piece has been prepared, transfer it to a well-heated, deep serving platter.

Peel the hot potatoes and cut into slices ½ inch thick. Arrange them around the skate.

Spoon the sauce over all (*see Note*) and sprinkle with parsley leaves. Serve immediately.

NOTE: *The coriander seeds impart flavor to the sauce, but when spooned over the fish, they seem somewhat excessive. If you wish, you can remove some of them just before serving. Ed.*

Saint-Pierre à la boulangère
FISH BAKED WITH POTATOES

To serve 4:

1 *Saint-Pierre,* about 3¼ pounds cleaned, but left whole (*see
Note*)

8 tablespoons butter, in all

6 large onions, halved and thinly sliced (*if using extra-large
"Spanish" onions, 4 will be sufficient; Ed.*)

1 large clove garlic, finely chopped

Coarse salt

Freshly ground pepper

2½ pounds Idaho potatoes

2 to 3 cups Chicken Stock (*fond blanc de volaille,* page 16)

Sprigs of fresh thyme (*or substitute ½ teaspoon dried thyme;
Ed.*)

NOTE: Saint-Pierre, *also called John Dory, is unavailable in the United
States. However, either striped bass or red snapper will adapt very
well to this recipe. I suggest that, rather than buying a whole 3¼-
pound fish, which, with the head included, will not be very large,
you buy a thick 2½- to 2¼-pound piece of a much larger fish. This
way, there will be no doubt about the fish and the potatoes being
properly cooked both at the same time. Ed.*

PREPARATION:

Preheat oven to 350° F.

Melt 6 tablespoons of butter in large frying pan (*or, if possible,
use the same pan in which the fish will be baked; Ed.*). Over moderate to low heat, sauté the onions in the butter without letting them
brown. Allow 20 to 30 minutes for this operation. When the onions
are done, spread them evenly over the bottom of a baking pan, or an
attractive *au gratin* dish. (*Bear in mind that the fish will be served
from the pan in which it is cooked. Ed.*) Scatter the garlic over all.
Rub the fish inside and out with salt and pepper, and lay it on top
of the onions.

Slice the potatoes as thin as possible, using a *mandoline* or other slicing device. Dry them well in a towel, then mix thoroughly with salt and pepper. Cover the fish entirely with potato slices, but heap most of the potatoes around the sides of the fish.

Bring the chicken stock to a boil and pour it over all. Sprinkle the potatoes with more salt and pepper and scatter the thyme over them. *(If using fresh thyme, rub the leaves from their branches evenly over the potatoes. Ed.)*

Melt the remaining 2 tablespoons of butter in a small saucepan and brush the potatoes with it. Cut a sheet of wax paper to fit the shape of the pan, rub it lightly with butter, and place it, butter side down, over the potatoes.

COOKING:

Bake the fish about 1 hour; the time depends on the potatoes. Frequently lift the wax paper, tilt the baking pan, and baste the potatoes with the broth. Make sure that the fish remains covered by them.

When the potatoes are done, if they have not absorbed all the juices, then carefully pour the juices off into a small saucepan. Boil them down over high heat until syrupy, and spoon the reduction back over the dish.

Serve the fish and potatoes directly from the pan in which they were cooked.

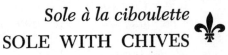

Sole à la ciboulette
SOLE WITH CHIVES
(Color picture 6)

To serve 4:
  4 sole, about ¾ pound each (*see Note*)
  Salt
  Freshly ground pepper
  8 tablespoons butter, clarified (*see directions below*)
  1 cup Fish Stock (*fumet de poisson*, page 20), in all
  3½ ounces (about 2 cups) dry bread crumbs without crust
  3 tablespoons dry vermouth
  ½ cup dry white wine

1 shallot, finely chopped
1 cup *crème fraîche* (page 22)
1 rounded teaspoon tomato paste
½ lemon
1 tablespoon butter
3 tablespoons chopped chives

NOTE: *In this country, the fish we call sole is really a type of flounder and is generally available only in fillets. Though the recipe can succeed with fish fillets, breading one side only as directed, substituting small, whole flounders would be the preferable way to prepare this dish. Ed.*

HAVE READY:

1. The sole: Remove the brown skin from the fish, scale the white side, and cut off the head on a diagonal. Season the sole well with salt and pepper. (*If substituting whole flounder, do not bother to remove the brown skin. Ed.*)

2. The clarified butter: *Place the butter in a small saucepan and melt it over the lowest possible heat. Skim off all of the white whey floating on the surface, then, carefully, pour off the clear golden liquid. Avoid all milky-white residue remaining in the bottom of the pan. Ed.*

3. Using a little softened butter, lightly grease a baking pan large enough to hold the fish side by side. Then add ½ cup of fish stock. (*Use either tin-lined copper, enameled cast iron, or flameproof glass or ceramic. Do not use aluminum. Ed.*)

COOKING THE SOLE:

Preheat oven to 425° F.

Pour the warm clarified butter into a deep plate. Roll the fish in it, one at a time, then dredge only the white-skin side in the bread crumbs. Lay the fish, crumb side up, in the prepared baking pan, taking care not to let the crumbs become moistened by the fish stock.

Dribble the remaining clarified butter over the bread crumbs, and place the fish in the oven for exactly 15 minutes. If the bread crumbs are not sufficiently browned in this time, run the fish briefly under a preheated broiler. Take care not to burn the crumbs or overcook the fish!

Use two large spatulas to lift the sole from the pan and arrange it on a heated platter. Carefully remove all small bones and fins from around the fish, then cover to keep warm.

PREPARATION OF THE SAUCE:

Over moderately high heat, add vermouth, wine, the remaining ½ cup of fish stock, and shallot to the baking pan. Boil down until the liquid has almost entirely evaporated. Then add the *crème fraîche* and stir in the tomato paste. Bring the sauce to a boil and cook, stirring constantly, until thickened. Add a delicate squeeze of lemon juice and taste for seasoning. The sauce will probably need salt.

Pass the sauce through a fine sieve (*optional*), return it to the stove, and keep hot over low heat. At the last moment stir in 1 tablespoon of butter to add gloss.

TO SERVE:

Distribute the sauce evenly in the centers of 4 large heated plates. Sprinkle liberally with chives, and rest the sole on top. Serve at once.

Filets de turbotin aux concombres
FILLET OF TURBOT WITH CUCUMBERS

To serve 4:
  1 *turbot*, about 2¾ pounds, to yield approximately 1¾ to 2 pounds fish fillets (*see Note*)
  1 to 2 cucumbers (*1 long European cucumber, or 2 of the standard variety; Ed.*)
  Butter
  2 shallots, finely chopped
  Salt
  Freshly ground pepper, preferably white
  ¾ cup dry white wine
  1 cup Fish Stock (*fumet de poisson*, page 20), prepared from the bones of the filleted fish if they are available
  2 cups *crème fraîche* (page 22)

Juice of ¼ lemon
1 tomato, peeled and diced
1 tablespoon coarsely chopped parsley

NOTE: Turbot *as known in Europe and intended for this recipe is not available in the United States. Substitute filleted striped bass or halibut. Ed.*

HAVE READY:

1. The cucumber: Choose a long firm cucumber. Divide it in half crosswise, then cut each half again into 3 short stumps. *(If standard cucumbers are used, adjust the divisions to equal approximately 1½-inch segments. Ed.)*

Peel the cucumber segments, then cut thin slices from all sides until you reach the seeds, which you discard. Now cut the slices into toothpick-size *julienne* strips. Soak them in a bowl of ice water for 8 to 10 hours.

2. The *turbot*: If your fish merchant has not prepared the *turbot*, cut the fillets in the following manner: Using a boning knife, trace a line down the center of the fish from the base of the head to the tail. On this groove, insert the knife blade until it hits the spine. Slip a plate beneath the fillet to catch the meat as you shave the knife across the dorsal bone. Repeat this procedure on the other side, obtaining 4 fillets (2 of them will be slightly smaller than the others). Remove the white and the black skins.

Cutting on a bias, divide the 2 large fillets into 4 pieces, and the smaller fillets into 2 pieces. This should create 12 diamond shapes, more or less regular in size.

COOKING:

Prepare a fish *fumet* from the bones of the *turbot*. Chop the head and skeleton into several pieces, using a meat cleaver, and place them in a casserole with 1½ cups water. Bring the liquid to a boil and simmer the bones for 20 minutes, then pass the *fumet* through a fine sieve.

Liberally butter the bottom of a long flameproof platter (*an oval tin-lined copper pan or* au gratin *dish will do nicely; Ed.*), and scatter the shallot over it. Season the fillets with salt and pepper and arrange them side by side in the platter or dish.

Moisten with white wine and cooled fish *fumet*. Cover the fillets with a sheet of buttered wax paper cut to the shape of the platter, and place over medium heat. Slowly bring the liquid to a boil, then lower the heat and poach the fish gently for about 6 minutes.

NOTE: *Both the fish suggested as substitutes for turbot will be of firmer flesh and greater thickness, therefore needing a slightly longer cooking time.*

Striped bass: Baste after 5 minutes, then poach approximately 5 minutes longer, depending on thickness.

Halibut: Using two large spatulas, carefully turn the halibut after 5 minutes, then poach 6 minutes longer, or until done. After turning the halibut, add a fresh piece of wax paper if necessary. Ed.

THE SAUCE:

Take the platter from the stove and carefully pour off all cooking liquid into a heavy medium-size saucepan. Boil down rapidly, until reduced by three-quarters. Add the *crème fraîche* and reduce again, until about ¾ cup remains. (*Watch that it does not boil over! Ed.*) Season the sauce with salt and pepper and a few drops of lemon juice.

Drain the cucumber *julienne* and plunge it, with the diced tomato, into a pan of boiling salted water. Cook 1 minute, drain in a sieve, and add it to the sauce.

TO SERVE:

Make sure that no liquid remains in the platter with the fillets; remove the wax paper and nap them with sauce, distributing the cucumber and tomato attractively over all.

Simmer 1 minute, then serve the fillets from the cooking platter with a sprinkling of chopped parsley.

Les volailles

POULTRY

Canette aux baies de cassis
DUCK WITH BLACK CURRANTS
(Color picture 14)

To serve 4:
  2 *Barbarie* ducks, about 3 pounds each dressed (*see Note*)
  Salt
  Freshly ground pepper
  1 tablespoon peanut oil
  10 ounces black currants, fresh or frozen, depending on the season
    (*see Note*)
  1½ tablespoons sugar
  ⅜ cup red wine vinegar
  1 tablespoon red currant jelly
  2½ tablespoons *crème de cassis* (black-currant liqueur)
  1½ cups Concentrated Veal Stock with Tomato (*demi-glace to-
    matée*, page 17)
  6 tablespoons butter

NOTE: *Try to find Muscovy ducks which are equivalent to the* canard
de Barbarie. *If they are not dressed, their weight will be about 4½
pounds each.*

In the United States it is unlikely that you will find fresh, or frozen, black currants marketed, though people do grow them and they can be found in the wild. However, they are available preserved in light syrup, imported from Poland and England. The English currants are slightly sweeter. Ed.

HAVE READY:

1. The ducks: preheat oven to 450° F.

Truss the ducks and season with salt and pepper. Place them in a heavy casserole, brush with peanut oil, and brown them on all sides over medium to high heat. Allow about 20 minutes for this operation, then finish the ducks in the oven.

Roast 25 minutes, turning them several times. When the roasting is completed, place the ducks on a carving platter and let them stand for at least 1 hour at room temperature. Pour off all fat remaining in the casserole, but do not wash it.

2. The black currants: If they are fresh, place them in a saucepan with ¼ cup water and 1½ tablespoons sugar. Simmer, covered, for 5 minutes. *(If the berries are preserved, drain a heaping cupful in a sieve. Reserve their juice. Ed.)*

CARVING THE DUCKS:

Place each duck on its back, untruss, and cut off the legs at the joint above the thigh. Then, using a sharp carving knife, make one long incision down the center, and scrape from the length of the breastbone down the rib cage until you reach the joint of the wing. Remove the large fillet in one piece and repeat on the other side.

In the same manner, disengage the *filet mignon* (the long strip which adheres to the carcass just below the breast). Using a heavy knife, chop off and discard the tail.

Cut the carcasses into manageable pieces. *(Use a meat cleaver or poultry shears for this operation. Ed.)*

PREPARATION OF THE SAUCE:

Deglaze the casserole in which the ducks were cooked with vinegar and, after a minute or two, add the red currant jelly. Boil until the juices caramelize, then stir in the *crème de cassis*.

Add the *demi-glace*, the carcasses of the ducks, and a scant ⅓ cup of the juice rendered from the cooked currants. *(If using preserved currants, add the same amount of syrup. Ed.)*

Bring to a boil, then reduce heat to very low. Let the sauce barely simmer for 20 minutes. During this time skim off any fat and impurities that rise to the surface.

Pass the sauce through a fine sieve into a small casserole, pressing down on the bones. Then, stir in the butter, a tablespoon at a time, to give it gloss, add the currants, and taste for seasoning. The sauce should be neither too sweet nor too salty.

TO SERVE:

Separate the drumstick and thigh sections of the legs at the joints above the drumsticks, and arrange them in a cross in the center of a hot, flameproof serving platter. Cut the fillets into 4 thin slices each, and arrange them, slightly overlapping, in a crown surrounding the legs.

Heat the platter for a few seconds on top of the stove, then nap with boiling sauce.

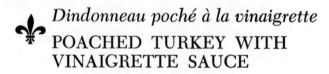

Dindonneau poché à la vinaigrette
POACHED TURKEY WITH VINAIGRETTE SAUCE

NOTE: *This dish is rather like a New England boiled dinner, but given the refreshing note of an accompanying vinaigrette sauce. Before purchasing the turkey, make sure you have available a 20-quart stockpot or other utensil of similar size. Ed.*

To serve 8: (*This recipe will serve 10 with a few additional vegetables. Ed.*)
  1 small fresh turkey, 8 to 10 pounds (6 or 7 pounds dressed)
  Chicken bones: necks, backs, feet, etc., to enrich the broth
  ½ lemon
  Coarse salt, about 3 tablespoons
  1 stalk celery with leaves

A few sprigs fresh thyme (*or substitute ½ teaspoon dried thyme; Ed.*)
1 bay leaf
8 leeks
8 small carrots
8 small turnips
1 large celery root (celeriac), about 1½ pounds, cut into approximately 16 sticks 3 inches long
½ to 1 whole cauliflower, divided into flowerets

THE *vinaigrette* SAUCE:

1 teaspoon imported *moutarde blanche,* or substitute Dijon mustard
A scant 3 tablespoons red wine vinegar
Coarse salt
Freshly ground pepper
⅓ cup walnut oil
2 truffles, cut into thin slivers, or substitute 1 tablespoon finely chopped fresh chervil or parsley

NOTE: *The proportions given here for the* vinaigrette *are not quite sufficient for 8 persons, but it is so quickly prepared that I suggest you make two bowls, which will also be convenient for serving. Ed.*

PREPARATION:

1. Truss the turkey and rub its skin with lemon to preserve the whiteness.
2. Prepare a *bouquet garni* composed of the celery, thyme, bay leaf, and the green tops of the leeks, tied together.

COOKING THE TURKEY:

Place the chicken bones at the bottom of the stockpot, then add the turkey, enough cold water to cover it completely, and a handful of coarse salt.

Bring the water to a boil and, after removing all scum from the surface, add the *bouquet garni.* Partially cover the stockpot and reduce the heat to a gentle simmer. Cook the turkey for 1 hour and 15 minutes. (*In timing your meal, be aware that it will take 30 minutes or more to bring the water to a boil. Ed.*)

PREPARATION OF THE SAUCE:

While the turkey is cooking, prepare the *vinaigrette*: In a small bowl, combine the mustard, vinegar, salt, and pepper. Slowly add the oil while beating vigorously with a small wire whisk. Do not add the truffles until the last minute before serving. If you are using chervil or parsley, it may be incorporated earlier.

COOKING THE VEGETABLES:

When the turkey has cooked for the hour and 15 minutes, add to the pot the white part of the leeks, tied together in bunches of 4, and all the other vegetables except the cauliflower. (The cauliflower will be boiled separately during the last 10 minutes of cooking.) Over high heat, return the broth to a boil, then reduce to a simmer. Continue to cook the vegetables and turkey, partially covered, for 20 to 30 minutes.

Ten minutes before the vegetables are ready, remove enough broth from the stockpot to cook the cauliflower. In a small saucepan, boil the flowerets in broth during these remaining 10 minutes.

TO SERVE:

Carefully lift the turkey from the stockpot and untruss it. Present the bird on a large platter surrounded by the vegetables before carving it. Add the truffles to the *vinaigrette* and pass it separately.

NOTE: *The vegetables, by themselves, are almost too much for one platter, let alone with the turkey on it as well. Since the whole poached turkey is not particularly attractive, I suggest keeping the vegetables warm while you carve the bird. Then serve both the turkey and the vegetables from two platters, with leeks and carrots dispersed on each for their color. Ed.*

Pigeon aux gousses d'ail en chemise
PIGEON WITH GARLIC SAUCE

(Color picture 7)

To serve 4:
  4 pigeons, dressed (livers reserved)
  7 tablespoons butter, in all
  Coarse salt
  Freshly ground pepper
  24 cloves garlic, unpeeled
  1 tablespoon *foie gras* (a good-quality tinned *foie gras* or *purée de foie gras* will suffice)
  2 tablespoons cognac
  ½ cup Chicken Stock (*fond blanc de volaille*, page 16)

PREPARATION:

1. Cut off the neck of each pigeon close to the body, then cut off the wing tips. Place 2 teaspoons of butter inside each bird and truss them, pulling the legs down tightly over the body. Season with salt and pepper.

2. Detach the cloves of garlic from the heads without removing the skins.

3. Rub the *foie gras* through a fine sieve into a small mixing bowl. Set it aside, leaving the sieve in place.

COOKING:

Preheat oven to 425° F.

Heat the remaining butter in a sauté pan and brown the pigeons slowly on all sides. Add the garlic, place the pan in the oven, and roast the pigeons 20 minutes, basting frequently.

Remove the pigeons from the oven and turn them out into another roasting pan with 8 cloves of garlic and the cooking butter. Keep them warm in the turned-off oven.

THE SAUCE:

Working quickly, add the reserved pigeon livers to the first roasting pan and sauté them briefly with the remaining 16 cloves of garlic.

Deglaze the pan with cognac and press everything through the fine sieve into the bowl with the *foie gras*. Discard the remnants of skin from the garlic, and mix the *foie gras*, liver, and garlic purée together until well blended. Add the chicken stock to the pan and bring to a boil, then thicken with the liver and garlic purée.

Untruss the pigeons and warm them gently in the sauce for 2 to 3 minutes. (*When returning the pigeons to the first pan, do not add any of the butter remaining in the other pan in which they were resting. Ed.*) Taste for seasoning.

TO SERVE:

Present the pigeons on a hot platter with the remaining 8 cloves of garlic scattered over them and napped with the sauce.

Accompany the pigeons with Crisp Ruffled Potatoes (*pommes gaufrettes au beurre*, page 201).

Pigeonneaux sable doré
SQUAB IN A GOLDEN CRUST

To serve 4:
    4 squab, dressed and trussed for cooking
    Coarse salt
    Freshly ground pepper
    3 teaspoons English powdered mustard
    ¾ cup dry white wine, in all
    Fresh bread crumbs
    10 tablespoons butter, in all
    2¼ pounds celery root (celeriac)
    ½ lemon
    1½ tablespoons cognac
    2 teaspoons Dijon mustard

1. The squab: Sprinkle the squab with salt and pepper. Mix the dry mustard with a scant 2 tablespoons of the wine and smear the birds with this paste. Then roll them in bread crumbs, pressing to make sure the crumbs adhere.

Melt 4 tablespoons of butter in a small skillet. Turn the squab in the butter until coated, then roll them again in bread crumbs. Set the birds aside.

2. The celery root: Peel the celery root, and trim it into large oval shapes, 2 inches long and 1½ inches thick. Rub the pieces of celery root with lemon to prevent them from darkening, and drop them into boiling salted water. After 8 minutes, drain the celery root and plunge it into a bowl of cold water. Then drain thoroughly in a sieve.

COOKING:

Preheat oven to 450° F.

Heat the remaining butter in a shallow casserole, or skillet, large enough to hold the squab and their *garniture*. When the butter begins to foam, add the squab, and brown them in the oven for 15 minutes.

Surround the birds with celery root, baste them well, and roast another 15 minutes.

Place the squab and celery root on a heatproof platter. Pour the butter from the casserole over them, as well as any crumbs that may have fallen off the birds during the roasting. Return them to the turned-off oven to keep warm.

PREPARATION OF THE SAUCE:

Deglaze the casserole with cognac and add the remaining white wine. Boil the wine over high heat until the liquid is reduced to the point of caramelization, barely coating the bottom of the casserole. Add ¼ cup of water and return the liquid to a boil. Stir in the mustard and reduce the heat to prevent further evaporation.

TO SERVE:

Untruss the squab, cut them in half, and arrange the halves on another, hot serving platter, surrounded by the celery root. Sprinkle lightly with salt and pepper and nap them with the mustard sauce. Their crust will resemble golden sand.

Poulet aux chicons
CHICKEN BRAISED WITH ENDIVES

To serve 4:
    1 roasting chicken, about 3½ pounds dressed
    2 pounds endives (*chicons*)
    Salt
    Freshly ground pepper
    Flour
    2 tablespoons butter
    2 cups *crème fraîche* (page 22)
    ¼ lemon

HAVE READY:

1. The chicken: Clean the bird and cut off the neck, tail, feet, and wing tips. Using poultry shears, split the chicken open along the backbone and cut off the vertebrae completely.

Spread the chicken open, pull out the small ribs covering the breast and, if you can, remove the entire breastbone, making sure not to cut through the chicken. You do not want to detach the two sides.

2. The endives: Cut the endives into large *julienne* strips, lengthwise. (*Do this by cutting them in half, then cut each half into thirds. Ed.*) Wash the endives and, after draining, dry them in a towel.

COOKING:

Season the chicken with salt and pepper and dust it lightly with flour.

Melt the butter in a large, heavy casserole that will hold the chicken comfortably (*or use a 12-inch skillet with a cover; Ed.*). Place the chicken in the butter, skin side down, and cook it slowly, until golden brown. (*Adjust the heat to be sure that it does not burn. Ed.*) Turn the chicken and cook the second side.

Place the endives around the chicken, cover the casserole and cook the endives with the chicken over low heat for 15 minutes to bring out their flavor.

Add the *crème fraîche* to the casserole and bring to a boil, uncovered. Reduce the heat to barely a simmer, re-cover the casserole, and continue cooking the chicken about 30 minutes, or until done.

To be certain that the chicken has finished cooking, prick the joint at the thigh with the point of a knife. The juices should run clear, not pink.

Taste the sauce for seasoning, adding a squeeze of lemon juice. Serve the chicken and endive from the casserole.

Poulet au vinaigre de vin
CHICKEN WITH VINEGAR SAUCE

To serve 4:
> One 3½-pound chicken, dressed
> Coarse salt
> Freshly ground pepper
> 1 onion, sliced
> 1 carrot, sliced
> 6 tablespoons butter, in all
> 15 large cloves garlic, unpeeled
> 3 tablespoons red wine vinegar
> 1 tablespoon tomato paste
> 2 ripe tomatoes, chopped
> *Bouquet garni* (sprigs of thyme and parsley and a bay leaf, tied
>   together)
> 1 tablespoon chopped seaweed, preserved in vinegar, or
>   1 tablespoon chopped fresh chervil

PREPARE THE CHICKEN:

After the chicken has been cleaned, cut it up in this manner: Detach the leg-thigh sections and cut apart legs from thighs. Remove the wings at the second joint, leaving the meaty part of the wing attached to the breast. Divide the breast into two parts lengthwise.

Season the breast, legs, and thighs with salt and pepper.

THE STOCK:

Place the carcass, wing tips, neck, feet (*if available*), and giblets in a medium-size casserole with the sliced onion and carrot. Add cold water to cover and bring to a boil. Boil the stock gently for 20 to 30 minutes. Strain the broth and skim off the fat.

COOKING THE CHICKEN:

Melt 2 tablespoons of butter in a heavy skillet large enough to hold all the chicken parts without overlapping. Arrange them in the pan, skin side down, and cook, uncovered, over medium to high heat for 5 minutes on each side, or until nicely browned.

Scatter the garlic around the chicken, and cook, covered, for 20 minutes over medium to low heat.

Holding the lid over the skillet to prevent the chicken from falling out, pour off all the fat and pan juices into a bowl. Then skim off the fat, reserving the juices that accumulate at the bottom of the bowl.

Leaving the chicken in the skillet, deglaze the skillet with the vinegar. Boil the vinegar until nearly evaporated, then add the reserved pan juices. Stir in the tomato paste and add the chopped fresh tomatoes and *bouquet garni*. Re-cover the skillet and simmer the chicken for another 10 to 15 minutes, then remove it and cover to keep warm.

PREPARATION OF THE SAUCE:

Add 2 cups of chicken broth to the skillet and boil it down until there is just enough sauce left to coat the chicken.

Over high heat, whisk in the remaining butter, a tablespoon at a time; the butter should create a thick *liaison*. Then, push the sauce through a coarse sieve, pressing down hard on the tomato pulp and garlic to release their juices. This will give the sauce a distinctive taste.

TO SERVE:

Arrange the chicken in a mound on a hot serving platter. Nap with sauce and sprinkle chopped seaweed, or chervil, over all.

Poulet aux herbes de province
CHICKEN WITH FRESH HERBS ⚜

NOTE: *The success of this unique dish lies in the use of massive quantities of fresh herbs. Though an herb, if unavailable, might possibly be omitted, dried herbs (except for the bay leaf), cannot be substituted. The leaves should be measured with their stems removed. Ed.*

To serve 4:

One 3½-pound chicken
3 cups (1¼ ounces) parsley leaves, loosely packed
2 cups (1 ounce) basil leaves, loosely packed
1 cup (½ ounce) tarragon leaves, loosely packed
¾ cup (⅓ ounce) chervil leaves, loosely packed
¾ cup (⅙ ounce) mint leaves, loosely packed
18 tablespoons (½ pound plus 2 tablespoons) butter, in all
Coarse salt
Freshly ground pepper
4 teaspoons lemon juice
1 cup rice
1 branch thyme
1 branch rosemary
1 sage leaf
1 small bay leaf

HAVE READY:

1. The herb butter: Wash the parsley, basil, tarragon, chervil, and mint leaves. Drain, and dry with paper towels. Finely chop ⅓ of these herbs and mix them with 12 tablespoons (1½ sticks), softened, of the butter. Add salt and pepper, and incorporate the lemon juice little by little. Mash the mixture with a fork until well blended.

2. The chicken: Clean, and singe the bird, then lay it on its back with the breast facing toward you. Carefully work the skin away from the neck, detaching it from the flesh just enough so that you can slip your fingers down the length of the breast. Take care not to tear the skin.

With a small sharp knife, make a groove separating the flesh from both sides of the breastbone, following the length of each fillet. Fill these 2 pockets with half the herb butter. Spread the remaining half under the skin. Season the chicken, inside and out, with salt and pepper, then truss.

3. The rice: Wash well in a sieve under running water and drain.

COOKING THE CHICKEN:

Melt the remaining 6 tablespoons of butter in the bottom of a heavy oval casserole. Lay the chicken on its side and, over medium to low heat, lightly brown it on one side, then the other. *(Do not lay the bird directly on its breast! Ed.)* This operation should take about 10 minutes. When finished, rest the chicken on its back, surrounded by the remaining herbs, including thyme, rosemary, sage, and bay leaf.

Cover the casserole and cook over very low heat (if necessary, use an asbestos pad) for about 1½ hours, or until done. Baste frequently during the course of cooking. The herbs will become an infusion in the juices; take care that they do not scorch.

COOKING THE RICE:

Preheat oven to 325° F.

Drain the rice and turn it into a large kettle of boiling salted water. Cook 10 minutes, then drain in a sieve, and rinse lightly. Place the sieve over a pan of simmering water to keep the rice warm. Fluff it up occasionally.

FINISHING THE CHICKEN AND THE RICE:

Untruss the chicken and place it on a deep hot platter. Remove the thyme, rosemary, sage, and bay leaf from the casserole and discard them. Spoon the remaining herbs, but not the juices, over the chicken.

Turn the rice out onto a hot, heatproof serving dish and moisten it with 8 tablespoons of the cooking butter skimmed off the top of the juices. Sprinkle the rice with salt, cover with a piece of wax paper, then place in the preheated oven for 15 minutes.

If the casserole juices are not already caramelized, reduce them without allowing them to burn. Then add ⅜ cup water in order to obtain a sufficient amount of good brown juice, which will have a slightly green cast. Reduce again to obtain just enough juice to serve 2 large spoonfuls per person.

TO SERVE:

Present the chicken breast side up, covered with herbs and moistened with the juices, before carving. Serve the rice separately.

Les viandes

MEATS

La bouillonnade

A VARIETY OF MEATS AND VEGETABLES POACHED IN BROTH

To serve 4:

> 7 ounces fillet of beef
> 6 ounces fillet of veal
> 1 boneless chicken breast, about 6 ounces
> Sprigs of fresh tarragon (*substitute parsley, if necessary; Ed.*)
> 4 sprigs white celery leaves, taken from the heart
> 2 to 3 carrots, depending on size
> 1 large leek, white part only
> 1 large onion
> 4 small fresh figs (in season)
> 1 quart strong Chicken Stock (*fond blanc de volaille*, page 16)
> 1 rounded teaspoon tomato paste
> 3 tablespoons red wine vinegar
> Salt
> Freshly ground pepper

This dish has the unusual touch of being prepared at the table by the guests. It is cooked in a *fondue* pot, placed in the center of the table so that each guest may cook his own meat and *garniture* in hot bubbling broth, according to his own taste and appetite.

133

HAVE READY:

1. The meats: Trim away all fat and cut the fillets of beef and veal into very thin medallions, about 1 ounce each.

Cut the chicken breast in slices as thin as possible. (*It helps immensely if the meats are partially frozen when you slice them. Ed.*)

Present the meats arranged in a circle on a porcelain or earthenware platter and decorated with sprigs of tarragon and celery leaves.

2. The vegetables: Peel the carrots, cut them in half and, using a *mandoline* or other cutting device, slice them thinly lengthwise.

Remove the exterior leaves of the leek, without splitting it in half, and cut the white part into 8 even rounds.

Cut the onion into thick, round slices.

Peel the figs, but leave them whole.

COOKING:

Place a saucepan, preferably a *fondue* pot, over an alcohol or other portable burner. Pour in hot chicken stock and add tomato paste and vinegar. Bring the broth to a boil, add the carrots and leeks, and cook 5 minutes.

Place the platter of meats on the table next to the *fondue* pot. Then add onion, figs, tarragon, and celery to the broth. After a moment, add half the chicken, and let it cook about 5 minutes, depending on the thickness of the slices. After 5 minutes, add half the veal, boil 1 minute, then follow with half the beef. Everything should now be ready within 1 minute.

Each guest, with the help of a fork and spoon, places a little bouillon, meat, and *garniture* on a deep plate.

When the first portion of meats has been depleted, add the remaining meat to the broth, timing the cooking the same way.

This dish brings life and cheer to an evening among friends.

Le coupe-jarret

FIVE COURSES FROM ONE KETTLE

(Color picture 11)

This dish is composed of 5 different meats, but all cut from the shank, each of which is served separately, one after the next, with its own *garniture* and sauce. All the meats except the chicken are served carved off the bone.

One must anticipate a long time for the preparation of this meal and guests with hearty appetites.

NOTE: *The sauces can be prepared a day in advance, but be fore-warned that 8 hours in all should be allowed from the beginning of the preparation of this dish to the time it is served. Ed.*

THE FIVE COURSES:

1. The first service: Pork hocks, accompanied by warm *flageolets* seasoned with a peanut-oil *vinaigrette*.

2. The second service: Veal shanks with a *garniture* of rice and a band of Fennel and Parsley Sauce spooned over the meat.

3. The third service: Beef shank surrounded by colorful vegetables. Pass mustard, *cornichons*, and a small bowl of coarse salt with the slices of beef.

4. The fourth service: Lamb shanks, generously napped with fresh tomato sauce.

5. The fifth service: Finish with chicken legs. Dress them with walnut-oil *vinaigrette* and scatter hot string beans over all.

To serve 8:

THE MEATS:

1 beef shank, about 4½ pounds
5 pork hocks, about 4 pounds
1 to 1½ veal shanks, about 2½ pounds
2 to 4 lamb shanks, about 2½ pounds (*see Note*)
8 chicken legs
4½ pounds beef bones

NOTE: *If lamb shanks are not available, substitute the shank end of a leg of lamb. Ed.*

THE GARNITURES:

3 pounds turnips (weight without tops)
1½ pounds carrots (weight without tops)
2¼ pounds hearts of celery
8 leeks, about 2½ pounds
½ pound dried *flageolets,* or other small white bean
½ pound young string beans
1 cup rice

THE SAUCES (double each recipe):

Fennel and Parsley Sauce (*sauce Albert Prost,* page 29)
Fresh Tomato Sauce (*coulis de tomates,* page 23)

TWO VINAIGRETTES:

½ cup red wine vinegar, in all
⅓ cup imported peanut oil
⅔ cup imported walnut oil
Salt
Freshly ground pepper
1 teaspoon Dijon mustard
1 tablespoon freshly chopped parsley
Fresh chervil leaves (*or substitute more parsley; Ed.*)

MISCELLANEOUS:

Salt
Coarse salt
Cheesecloth
1 carrot
1 onion, stuck with 2 cloves
2 *bouquets garnis* (sprigs of thyme and parsley and a bay leaf, tied together)
2 large onions, halved
1 whole unpeeled head of garlic, stuck with 4 cloves
4 tablespoons butter
1 small onion, finely chopped

CONDIMENTS:

Dijon mustard
Cornichons (tiny imported sour pickles)

PREPARATION OF THE MEATS:

Have your butcher trim the meats completely of fat, leaving a small handle of bone at one end of each shank (*see Note*). Tie the meat of each shank together securely with string, leaving an excess of about 20 inches from the knot to tie to the handle of the kettle; this will help to retrieve them out of the pot for serving.

Do the same with the chicken legs, except that they may be strung together like a necklace with 1 or 2 strings, rather than 8, to anchor them to the handle of the kettle.

NOTE: *Because of the way our meat is normally cut, it is unlikely that your butcher will be able to provide you with a handle of bone at the end of every shank. Though it facilitates carving the meat, it is not important. Ed.*

THE VEGETABLE GARNITURE:

Using a small sharp knife, peel and trim the turnips into 24 pieces the shape of fat corks. Peel and trim the carrots into pieces of similar size.

Cut the celery into 24 sticks, 2½ inches in length, or, if you have 6 hearts, quarter them. Use only the white part of the leeks, trim, and leave them whole.

Set the vegetables aside in ice water until ready to proceed with their cooking. *If you wish, you can also tie them in their separate cheesecloth sacks (see page 139) at this time. Ed.*

PREPARATION OF THE DRIED BEANS:

Soak the beans for 3 hours in warm water; drain, and place them in a large saucepan with enough cold water to cover them by ⅓ their volume.

Add 1 carrot, 1 onion stuck with 2 cloves, 1 *bouquet garni*, and a large pinch of coarse salt. Bring the beans to a simmer and skim off the foam that rises to the surface, then cook over low heat until tender. The length of time depends on the variety and quality of the beans.

THE STRING BEANS:

Trim the ends and cook them according to the classic method (page 184). Cook the beans from 3 to 8 minutes, depending upon their size, and refresh them as directed. They should be somewhat crunchy to the bite. They are to be reheated at the last moment before serving.

PREPARATION OF THE *vinaigrettes*:

1. *Vinaigrette* sauce for the dried beans: In a small mixing bowl, blend 1 teaspoon of Dijon mustard with 3 tablespoons vinegar, salt, and pepper. Then slowly beat in 6 tablespoons (⅓ cup) peanut oil, a little at a time. Do not mix the *vinaigrette* with the beans until just before serving. At that time, add 1 tablespoon chopped parsley.

2. *Vinaigrette* sauce for the chicken: Mix 5 tablespoons vinegar with salt and pepper, then slowly beat in 12 tablespoons (⅔ cup) walnut oil. At the last moment before serving, add a good pinch of coarsely chopped chervil leaves. (*If the taste of walnut oil is stronger than you like, use half walnut oil and half imported olive oil. Ed.*)

PREPARATION OF THE RICE:

The rice should be prepared about 40 minutes before the meats are finished—in other words, 20 minutes after you add the lamb shanks to the other meats.

Preheat oven to 450° F.

Melt the butter in a sauté pan and add the chopped onion. Cook the onion, covered, over low heat for 2 minutes, then add the rice with 1½ cups of boiling salted water. Lower the heat and cover the rice with a circle of wax paper cut to fit the circumference of the pan. Then cover with a lid and bake the rice in the oven for 18 minutes. After 18 minutes, remove the rice from the oven and let stand at room temperature, covered, for 20 minutes.

Uncover the pan and separate the grains of rice with a fork. Recover and return to the turned-off oven until ready to serve.

COOKING THE MEATS AND VEGETABLE *garniture*:

Cooking time for each meat and the vegetables:
  Beef: 5 hours
  Pork: 1½ hours
  Veal: 1½ hours

Lamb: 1 hour
Chicken: 30 minutes
Vegetables: 20 minutes

Fill a large 20- to 30-quart stockpot half full of salted water (*about 12 quarts water and 3 tablespoons coarse salt; Ed.*), then add the beef shank, and fill the empty space with beef bones. Bring the water to a simmer (*this will take at least 45 minutes; Ed.*) and cook the beef, uncovered, for 2 hours. Skim the surface from time to time, removing any grease and scum. (*By the time all the meats have finished cooking, there will have been about 1 quart of fat and impurities skimmed from the surface. Ed.*)

After 1½ hours, preheat oven to 475° F.

Roast the 4 onion halves on a dry baking sheet until lightly browned. Then, when the beef shank has cooked for 2 hours, add the roasted onions, 1 *bouquet garni*, and the whole head of garlic stuck with 4 cloves. Raise the heat to a gentle boil, bubbling only around the edges of the surface of the broth.

After the beef shank has cooked for 3½ hours (*1½ hours after adding the onions and spices; Ed.*), remove the beef bones, but not the shank, and fill the space with pork hocks and veal shanks.

After 4 hours (*30 minutes after adding the pork and veal; Ed.*), add the lamb shanks. After they have cooked for 30 minutes, add the chicken legs and, 10 minutes later, the vegetable *garniture* (turnips, carrots, celery, and leeks), each tied together in separate cheesecloth sacks. Cook the vegetables 20 minutes. (*Leave the same excess length of string attached to the sacks as for the meats, so that they may be easily retrieved when the vegetables are to be served. Ed.*)

At the end of this time, 5 hours after the beef shank first reached a simmer, everything should be perfectly cooked. (*Remember that the meats and vegetables remaining in the broth while the courses before them are being served will continue to cook even though the kettle is removed from heat. However, if you wish, you can stop or slow the cooking by adding 1 or more cups of cold water. Ed.*)

Serve the 5 courses in the order described on page 135. (*Strain and save the delicious broth for other uses. Ed.*)

Canon d'agneau aux fèves
SADDLE OF LAMB WITH FRESH WHITE BEANS

To serve 4:

1 saddle of lamb, about 4½ pounds (*because of the way meat is cut in the United States, the weight will be about 5½ pounds; Ed.*)

2¼ pounds fresh beans, unshelled (*use any fresh white bean, such as fava, lima, or butter beans; Ed.*)

5 tablespoons butter, in all

Coarse salt

Freshly ground pepper

1 shallot, chopped

½ cup dry white wine

1 scant cup heavy cream

PREPARATION:

1. Using a sharp boning knife, remove the 2 large fillets from the saddle, making the knife follow closely against the bone. Turn the saddle and take out the 2 small *filets mignons* found on the inner side of the bone.

2. Using the sharpest knife possible, remove the sinews from the larger fillets, leaving a thin layer of fat on the leaner side. Remove the transparent skin covering the *filets mignons*.

NOTE: *In this country either a saddle or rack of lamb (half a saddle) is sold with a "flap" attached to the larger fillet by a ridge of fat. Remove this flap and discard it or reserve it for another use. If it is wrapped around the large fillet, it will interfere with the proper cooking of this choice piece of meat. The flap also accounts for the difference in weight mentioned earlier. Ed.*

3. Break the bones into small sections—a procedure that is extremely difficult without a meat cleaver. If necessary, have your butcher do the entire boning operation for you.

4. Shell the beans and, depending upon the type of bean available, remove the exterior skin if there is one; this is the case with fava beans.

COOKING:

There are two separate procedures for the different fillets.

1. Roasting the large fillets: Preheat oven to 500° F.

Melt 3 tablespoons butter in a large, shallow and heavy casserole (*or cast-iron skillet; Ed.*). Season the fillets with salt and pepper and lay them over the melted butter. Fill the open spaces in the casserole with the broken bones.

Place the casserole in the hot oven for 4 minutes, then turn the meat carefully, without piercing the flesh, and roast it 4 minutes on the second side.

Remove the meat from the oven and leave it at room temperature, uncovered. (It is best to invert a plate over a larger plate and then to place the meat on top of both to catch the juices and to stop the cooking completely so that the meat does not stew in its own juice.)

2. Sautéing the smaller fillets: Drain the cooking butter from the large casserole into a small, heavy skillet. (*Do not rinse the casserole or discard the bones. Ed.*) Reheat the butter until sizzling, season the smaller fillets with salt and pepper, and cook them exactly 2 minutes on each side. Set them aside on the inverted plate with the larger fillets.

THE SAUCE:

Discard all remaining cooking fat from the large casserole without removing the bones, then add the shallot. Cover the casserole and cook the shallot 2 minutes over low heat to release its juices.

Pour in the white wine and raise the heat. Boil it, uncovered, to deglaze the casserole and, when the wine is greatly reduced, add the cream. Boil gently until the cream has thickened the sauce, then lower the heat, and taste for seasoning. Add salt and pepper, if necessary, and any lamb juices that have accumulated on the large plate under the fillets.

THE FRESH BEANS:

At the same time that you begin the sauce, drop the beans into boiling salted water and cook them for 5 minutes. Drain well, then sauté them in a small skillet with the remaining 2 tablespoons of butter.

TO SERVE:

Cut the fillets into slices ½ inch thick and arrange them in a circle on a warm serving platter, slightly overlapping, to form a crown.

Fill the center of the crown with the beans and nap the slices of lamb with a little of the sauce. Serve the remainder of the sauce separately.

Épaule de chevreau aux oignons nouveaux

ROAST SHOULDER OF KID (YOUNG GOAT) WITH SPRING ONIONS

To serve 4:

    2 shoulders of young goat, about 2 pounds (*see Note*)
    Coarse salt
    Freshly ground pepper
    10 spring onions, about 1 pound (*see Note*)
    7 tablespoons butter, in all
    ½ cup dry white wine
    ½ cup Concentrated Veal Stock with Tomato (*demi-glace tomatée*, page 17)
    20 fresh tarragon leaves (*or substitute 1 teaspoon dried tarragon; Ed.*)

NOTE: *Goat is frequently obtainable from Cuban, Puerto Rican, and other Latin butcher shops* (carnicerías). *And, it can sometimes be found around Easter, sold by Italian butchers.*

This dish may also be prepared with a leg of goat, given a slightly longer cooking time, or a leg of lamb, cooked considerably longer, depending on size. Both meats should be served "pink." In either case, add the onions 25 minutes before you expect the meat to be done.

Spring onions are sold like scallions; the difference lies in their round bulbous shape. Ed.

HAVE READY:

1. The goat: It is essential that the goat be young and of the best quality. Also, it should be aged 3 to 4 days.

Do not have the meat boned. Season it well with salt and pepper.

2. The onions: Choose white new onions. Peel them, leaving 2½ inches of green stem. Quarter them, remove the root end, and pull the onions apart with your fingers, separating them into thin sheets. It is these separated layers of the onions that give the dish its character.

COOKING:

Preheat oven to 450° F.

Melt 3½ tablespoons of butter in a shallow roasting pan and brown the shoulders evenly on all sides over medium to high heat.

Place the meat in the oven for 10 minutes, then surround it with the onions, and roast 25 minutes longer. Remove the meat and onions from the pan, arrange on a platter, and return them to the turned-off oven to keep warm.

Add the white wine to the roasting pan and deglaze over high heat. When the wine has nearly evaporated, add ¾ cup of water, then the *demi-glace*. Reduce for 10 minutes, or until only about ½ cup of sauce remains.

Return the shoulders to the pan, with the onions, and simmer a few minutes, taking care not to crush the onions. Stir the remaining 3½ tablespoons of butter, cut into tiny pieces, into the sauce to form a *liaison*. Add the fresh tarragon and taste for seasoning.

TO SERVE:

This dish should be eaten boiling hot, so attend to the carving of the meat as quickly as possible, then spoon the sauce and onions over all. Have heated serving plates ready to receive the meat.

Accompany this dish with Potatoes Roasted with Bacon (*pommes de terre "Mère Carles,"* page 202).

Les corsus de veau aux graines de moutarde
LOIN OF VEAL WITH MUSTARD SEEDS

To serve 4:
> 1¼ pounds boneless loin of veal, completely trimmed (*see Note*)
> Coarse salt
> Freshly ground pepper
> 4 tablespoons mustard seeds
> 3 rounded teaspoons Dijon mustard
> 3 tablespoons peanut oil
> 3½ tablespoons butter, in all
> 3 tablespoons Concentrated Veal Stock with Tomato (*demi-glace tomatée*, page 17)
> 1 rounded teaspoon imported tarragon mustard

In the *patois* of our region, *corsus* means stinginess. The veal is served in small scallops weighing roughly 1¾ ounces each, hence the idea so to name this recipe.

PREPARATION OF THE VEAL:

Have your butcher cut the veal into 16 scallops across the grain. (*If loin of veal is not available, veal cut from the rump, as used for* scaloppine, *can work successfully. Ed.*)

Season the meat lightly with salt and pepper, and place the scallops, spread out, between two sheets of wax paper. Flatten the veal with the side of a meat cleaver until the pieces are ⅛ inch thick and approximately 5 inches by 3 inches in size.

Lift off the top sheet of wax paper and cover one side of the veal with mustard seeds, pressing to help the coating adhere.

Reapply the wax paper and use it to help turn over the scallops. Lift the wax paper from the second side and smear it with Dijon mustard.

NOTE: *The success of this recipe now depends upon the seed-coated side of the veal becoming evenly browned. Since the scallops will shrink as they cook, you can begin by browning the first side in several skillets, and then consolidate them in one large pan to cook the second side. Ed.*

COOKING:

Heat the oil with 1½ tablespoons of butter in a large (*12-inch*), heavy skillet. When it begins to smoke, add the scallops, seed side down, without overlapping. Cook them for 1 minute, then turn the meat, and cook 1 minute longer on the second side.

Remove the scallops from the skillet and keep them warm on a hot plate covered with an inverted plate (*or with aluminum foil; Ed.*).

Drain the excess fat from the pan without disturbing any particles that may stick to the bottom. Deglaze the skillet with ½ cup of water and boil it until reduced by two-thirds. Add the *demi-glace* and reduce the liquid again until only 2 tablespoons remain.

Return the scallops to the skillet with their accumulated juices. Cover, and reheat them gently without letting the sauce return to a boil. (If it is allowed to boil, the meat will become tough!)

TO SERVE:

When ready to serve, arrange the scallops, seed side up, on a hot platter, slightly overlapping.

Mix the tarragon mustard with the pan juices and, over moderate heat, stir in the remaining butter, cut into tiny pieces.

Nap the *corsus* with the sauce and serve at once with Fried Pumpkin Cakes (*palets au potiron*, page 200).

Côte de veau cressonnière

VEAL CHOPS WITH WATERCRESS SAUCE

To serve 4:
    7 ounces watercress, 1½ to 2 bunches
    4 veal chops, about 6 ounces each
    Coarse salt
    Freshly ground pepper
    4 tablespoons butter
    1 large shallot, finely chopped
    2 cups *crème fraîche* (page 22)
    Juice of ½ lemon

HAVE READY:

1. The watercress: Remove all stems from the watercress, except for 4 sprigs to be reserved for decoration. Wash and drain the leaves.

2. The veal chops: The chops should be cut from between the second and fifth ribs. Sprinkle each side with salt and pepper.

COOKING THE CHOPS:

Melt the butter in a heavy skillet over medium heat. The skillet should be just large enough to hold the chops side by side (*about 10 inches in diameter and with a cover; Ed.*). When the butter begins to color slightly, arrange the chops within.

Cook the veal chops 15 to 20 minutes, or until thoroughly browned on each side. Take care to adjust the heat so that they do not burn, and turn them several times during the cooking. Remove the chops to a hot plate and cover to keep warm.

PREPARATION OF THE SAUCE:

Add the shallot to the cooking juices and cook, covered, over very low heat for 2 minutes. Do not allow it to brown.

Deglaze the pan with ¼ cup water, then add the watercress, and *crème fraîche*. Bring the *crème fraîche* to a gentle boil over medium to low heat, then cover the skillet tightly, and reduce heat to barely a simmer. Cook the sauce for 12 minutes.

Taste for seasoning (*it will probably need more salt and pepper; Ed.*), then add a good squeeze of lemon juice. Return the chops to the skillet, and simmer 3 minutes, basting continuously with sauce.

TO SERVE:

Turn the chops out onto a hot platter and nap with sauce. Then decorate with the reserved sprigs of watercress. Accompany the veal chops with rice (page 138).

Émincé de rognons de veau aux haricots blancs
VEAL KIDNEYS WITH WHITE BEANS

To serve 4:
 4 veal kidneys, about 8 ounces each
 1 pound fresh white beans, unshelled
 Salt
 Freshly ground pepper
 2 tablespoons butter
 1 shallot, finely chopped
 ⅝ cup Beaujolais Villages (or other light, dry red wine)
 ½ cup Concentrated Veal Stock with Tomato (*demi-glace tomatée,*
  page 17)
 1 cup *crème fraîche* (page 22)
 1 heaping teaspoon Dijon mustard
 2 tablespoons chopped parsley

HAVE READY:

1. The kidneys: Pull away all excess fat without removing the fine transparent membrane covering the kidneys. Make a cut lengthwise down the center of each one, and remove all the large inner sinews.
2. The white beans: Shell the beans and drop them into boiling salted water for 5 minutes. Drain and set aside. (*If beans such as favas are used, remove the exterior skin, which would shrivel when cooked. Ed.*)

COOKING:

Preheat oven to 450° F.

Season the kidneys with salt and pepper, then melt the butter in a skillet, and arrange them in the pan, one next to the other. Brown the kidneys on all sides, then place in the hot oven for 5 minutes to finish cooking.

Remove the kidneys from the skillet, drain on paper towels, and cover to keep warm. Add the shallot to the skillet and cook, covered, over low heat for 1 minute to release its juices. Add the wine and deglaze the pan over high heat. Boil until the wine is slightly reduced, then add the *demi-glace*. Cook until reduced by half.

Stir in the *crème fraîche* and boil gently until the sauce is slightly thickened.

FINISHING THE KIDNEYS:

In a small bowl, thin the mustard with 2 to 3 tablespoons of sauce, then blend it back into the rest of the sauce, and reduce heat to a simmer. Taste for seasoning.

Cut the kidneys into slices ½ inch thick and add them to the sauce with the beans. Heat together for 3 minutes without letting the sauce return to a boil; if it boils, the kidneys will toughen.

Sprinkle parsley over all and serve immediately.

Sauté de veau aux poireaux
VEAL SAUTÉ WITH LEEKS

To serve 4:
   1¾ pounds boneless veal, cut from the leg
   1¾ pounds leeks, white part only (*about 2 bunches*)
   3½ ounces (a scant cup) yellow raisins
   3 tablespoons butter
   ⅜ cup imported peanut oil
   Coarse salt
   Freshly ground pepper
   ½ cup dry white wine
   Bouquet garni (sprigs of thyme and parsley and a bay leaf, tied
      together)
   ¾ cup milk
   Juice of ½ lemon

HAVE READY:

1. Cut the veal into 2-inch cubes, about 1½ ounces each. (*This should yield approximately 4 pieces per person. Ed.*)
2. Cut the leeks into thin even slices.
3. Soak the raisins in cold water 1 hour or longer.

COOKING:

Heat the butter with the oil in a heavy copper pan, or enameled cast-iron skillet, large enough to hold the pieces of meat side by side. Season the veal with salt and pepper and arrange in the pan. Brown the meat, slowly, on each side, allowing about 15 minutes in all. Use tongs to turn the veal without piercing it.

Lower heat and add the leeks. Cook, covered, 10 minutes to release their juices. Stir once or twice, and make sure they do not brown. Add wine and *bouquet garni*, bring to a simmer, then add milk. Cook 1 hour, partially covered, stirring frequently. The sauce should thicken by itself.

FINISHING THE VEAL:

When the meat is tender, remove the *bouquet garni* and add the raisins, well drained, with a few drops of lemon juice.

Taste for seasoning, simmer a few minutes, and serve.

Tendrons de veau braisés aux salsifis
BRAISED BREAST OF VEAL WITH SALSIFY

To serve 4:

One 3-pound breast of veal (*this is roughly half a whole breast; Ed.*)

2 pounds salsify, or oyster plant (*see Note*)

½ cup distilled white vinegar

5 ounces lean salt pork (unsmoked bacon), in one piece

3 tablespoons butter

20 small white onions, peeled

Salt

Freshly ground pepper

Flour

1 quart hot Chicken Stock (*fond blanc de volaille*, page 16)

Bouquet garni (sprigs of thyme and parsley and a bay leaf, tied together)

1 tablespoon each chopped fresh chervil and parsley (*or use 2 tablespoons parsley; Ed.*)

NOTE: *Salsify, also called oyster plant, usually appears in late spring. Don't be put off by their pencil-like slimness; this is the way they should be, though it makes them tedious to clean. If you do not find salsify, young parsnips have a similar taste and can be substituted. If this is necessary, 1 pound of parsnips will be sufficient. Try to choose the smallest and most delicate possible. Ed.*

HAVE READY:

1. The veal breast: Have your butcher divide the breast into 4 equal pieces.

2. The salsify: Using a vegetable peeler, peel the salsify, then cut them into 2-inch sticks, and drop them into a large bowl of acidulated water. *(The vinegar helps to prevent them from turning brown. Ed.)*

3. The *lardons*: Cut the salt pork into pieces approximately 1½ inches long and ¼ inch thick. Put them in a small pan and cover with cold water. Bring the water to a boil and simmer 3 minutes. Drain, refresh them with cold water, drain again, and dry with paper towels.

COOKING:

Put the *lardons* in a heavy skillet or casserole (preferably cast iron) large enough to hold the pieces of veal side by side without over-lapping. Add the butter to the *lardons* and brown them lightly on all sides. Remove with a perforated spoon and set aside.

Add the onions to the skillet and brown them in the fat rendered from the salt pork. Then remove and set aside.

Season the pieces of veal with salt and pepper, dust with flour, and arrange them in the skillet to brown. The heat should be low to moderate. Allow about 20 minutes for this operation, turn the meat frequently, and adjust the heat as necessary. Remove the veal and set it aside with the onions and *lardons*. Do not clean the skillet.

Preheat oven to 350° F.

Rinse and dry the salsify and sprinkle with salt and pepper. Add them to the skillet used to cook the veal and brown them slowly. Allow 20 minutes for this, turning the salsify frequently.

Return the meat, onions, and *lardons* to the skillet. Add the hot chicken stock and *bouquet garni*, and bring to a boil. Cover the skillet tightly and place it in the oven. Cook 25 minutes, then reduce the oven temperature to 325° F. and cook 1 hour longer.

Return the skillet to the top of the stove and remove the *bouquet garni*. Bring the broth to a boil, uncovered, and cook for 3 minutes. Skim off the fat that rises to the surface with a large spoon.

TO SERVE:

Add the chervil and parsley and taste for seasoning. Arrange the pieces of veal on a large hot platter, slightly overlapping. Cover the meat with onions, *lardons*, and salsify.

Boil down the liquid remaining in the skillet until brown and syrupy, pour it over the *garniture*, and serve.

Tête de veau amourette

CALF'S HEAD WITH TOMATOES AND OLIVES

To serve 8:

1 calf's head, including tongue and brain (*see Note*)
8 ounces veal spinal marrow (*amourette*), if available
Salt
1 tablespoon distilled white vinegar
1 pound new potatoes
1 scant cup green olives
5 large tomatoes
3½ tablespoons olive oil
1 large onion, finely chopped
1 large carrot, finely chopped
3½ tablespoons cognac
½ cup dry white wine
1½ cups Concentrated Veal Stock with Tomato (*demi-glace to-matée*, page 17)
Bouquet garni (sprigs of thyme and parsley and a bay leaf, tied together)
Flour
1½ tablespoons butter
1½ tablespoons wine vinegar
Freshly ground pepper
2 to 3 tablespoons chopped parsley

NOTE: *The Troisgros' original recipe serves 4 persons and calls for 1 pound boneless meat from the calf's head, 4 ounces calf's tongue, and 4 ounces spinal marrow. In the United States, it is usually necessary to buy the entire calf's head, which can weigh up to 14 pounds.*

In this case, the tongue will be about 1¼ pounds and the pair of brains will weigh roughly 8 ounces. Do not be overwhelmed by the size of the head, as there will only be about 2 pounds of boneless meat. Spinal marrow is extremely difficult to come by, but fortunately it is of the same taste, character, and consistency as the calf's brain. Simply substitute the brain for the marrow. Prepare it, from soaking to cooking, exactly as directed for marrow.

Have your butcher split the head in half, clean it, removing the eyes, and, for convenience, cut it in half again. Though boning is a tedious job, I found it easiest to do after the initial blanching. Ed.

HAVE READY:

1. The calf's head and tongue: *(Scrub them well with a brush, then soak for several hours in cold water. Change the water occasionally. Ed.)*

Place the meats in a large kettle, cover with fresh cold water, add a handful of salt, and bring the water slowly to a boil over medium heat. Blanch the meats for 45 minutes, then drain, rinse off the scum, and refresh them in a basin of cold water. *(Have your kitchen sink free for this purpose. Ed.)* When chilled, drain again in a colander.

Peel the tongue and remove the outer skin of the calf's head, then remove every bit of meat and cartilaginous matter from the head. Discard the bones and trimmings, and cut the meats into pieces of about 3 ounces each.

2. The marrow: Soak the marrow *(or the brain)* in ice water for 1 hour or longer. Then, pull off any skin and traces of blood, and place in a saucepan of cold salted water to which the distilled vinegar has been added. Bring to a simmer *(not a boil)*, then lower heat, and cook just below a simmer for 15 minutes. Drain, and plunge into ice water. *(Do not soak; as soon as it is chilled, drain, and place in the refrigerator. Ed.)*

3. The potatoes: Peel and quarter them and trim each piece into the shape of a large cork. *(Do this just before they are to be added to the meat. Ed.)*

4. The olives: Pit the olives and place them in a saucepan. Cover with cold water and bring to a boil. Simmer 1 minute, drain in a sieve, and rinse with cold water.

5. The tomatoes: Drop them into boiling water. Count to 10, drain, and plunge immediately into cold water. Peel, then chop them coarsely.

COOKING:

Heat the olive oil in a large heavy casserole and brown the pieces of blanched calf's head meat and tongue. Stir constantly with a wooden spoon, scraping off the thin skin of meat glaze that will adhere to the bottom and sides of the casserole. This should take about 25 minutes.

Add the *mirepoix* of onion and carrot. Cover the casserole, lower heat, and cook 5 minutes to release their juices.

Deglaze the casserole with cognac and reduce slightly. Add the white wine, bring to a boil, then add the tomatoes, followed by the *demi-glace*. Add the *bouquet garni*, cover, and simmer 1 hour. After 30 minutes, set the cover of the casserole askew and, if necessary, increase the heat to maintain a simmer.

At the end of 1 hour, add the potatoes, and cook 30 minutes longer.

Cut the marrow (*or brain*) into pieces 2½ inches long. Dip lightly in flour and brown them in a skillet with 1½ tablespoons of butter. When browned, deglaze the skillet with wine vinegar.

TO FINISH:

Remove the *bouquet garni* from the casserole, and add the marrow, vinegar, and olives. Season liberally with pepper. Simmer about 10 minutes, then add a good handful of freshly chopped parsley. Serve very hot.

NOTE: *Hot mustard and* cornichons *(tiny sour pickles) are a nice accompaniment to* tête de veau *and, if the dish has been carefully skimmed of fat during the cooking, it is excellent served cold, in its own aspic, with the same condiments. Ed.*

Côte de boeuf au Fleurie
PRIME RIBS OF BEEF WITH MARROW AND WINE SAUCE

To serve 4:
  2 prime ribs of beef in one piece, about 3 pounds completely
     trimmed (see below)
  4 ounces beef marrow, removed from the bone (*see Note*)
  Coarse salt

Freshly ground pepper
8 tablespoons butter, in all
2 shallots, finely chopped (preferably the gray variety—*échalotes grises*)
1 cup Beaujolais de Fleurie (or other light, dry red wine)
4 rounded teaspoons Meat Glaze (*glace de viande*, page 18)

HAVE READY:

1. The beef: Ask your butcher to cut the meat from the first 2 ribs all the way to the bone of the 3rd rib and to make a handle by trimming the end of the bone very closely. Every bit of excess fat should be removed. (*Because meat in the United States is cut differently from meat in France, the bone that would become the handle has usually been previously removed. Ed.*)

2. The marrow: Purchase the marrow the day before and firm it in ice water overnight.

NOTE: *I found it easier to poach the marrow in the bone, keep it warm in the cooking liquid, and extract it from the bone just before serving. Two whole beef shinbones, sawed into manageable pieces, should give you the right amount. Ed.*

COOKING THE MEAT:

Season the *côte de boeuf* liberally with salt and pepper. Plan to cook the meat in either a heavy tin-lined copper sauté pan or a well-seasoned, cast-iron skillet. The pan should be just large enough to hold the meat.

Heat 3 tablespoons of the butter in the pan and, when it sizzles, put in the meat. Cook over high heat for 15 minutes on each side, basting frequently with the pan juices. Then turn the meat again, and cook 5 minutes longer on each side.

Place the meat on a warm plate, inverted over a larger plate, so that it will not stew in its own juices. The cooking time is calculated to allow a 20-minute rest period for the meat at room temperature.

POACHING THE MARROW:

While the meat rests, poach the chilled marrow. Cut it into slices ½ inch thick and place them in a small saucepan. Cover with cold salted water and bring slowly to a boil. Just as a faint simmer is reached, remove the saucepan from the heat, and set aside. Do not drain the marrow until you are ready to serve it.

NOTE: *If you are poaching the marrow in the bone, skim the surface of the water thoroughly, and let the marrow cook, just below a simmer, for 15 minutes. Ed.*

PREPARATION OF THE SAUCE:

Pour off just enough fat from the frying pan to coat the bottom of a medium-size heavy saucepan. Add the shallots and cook a few minutes, covered, over low heat to release their juices.

Deglaze the saucepan with red wine, raise the heat, and add the *glace de viande.* Cook the sauce until it is reduced by half, stirring frequently. Over very low heat, slowly beat in the remaining butter, cut into tiny pieces, a little at a time. Keep the sauce warm, but it must not reach a simmer again or it will separate, and you will have to add cold water to bring it back together again.

Taste for seasoning and pass the sauce through a fine sieve (*optional*).

TO SERVE:

Return the meat to the skillet it was cooked in and warm it on each side in the remnants of cooking fat. Then place it on a hot serving platter. Incorporate any juices rendered while the meat was resting into the wine sauce.

Drain the marrow, and dry it lightly with paper towels, then arrange the pieces on the meat, and pour the wine sauce over all. Cut the beef into 8 slices, parallel to the bone, and spoon the sauce over them.

Serve immediately on very hot plates and accompanied by Potatoes Cooked in Cream (*gratin de pommes de terre à la forézienne,* page 197).

Entrecôte dix sur dix
RIB STEAK TEN ON TEN

NOTE: *This recipe is so named because the steaks are cooked 10 seconds on each side. In France, the meat for this recipe is taken from between the 3rd and 4th ribs of beef. The beef is then boned and trimmed and cut into slices ¼ inch thick.*

If you have difficulty in finding an accommodating butcher to cut the entrecôte *as required, the recipe can still succeed with normal rib steaks (sometimes called club steaks), because it is the interesting onion sauce that is the focal point.*

If it is necessary to make this adjustment, cook ¾- to 1-inch steaks 2 minutes on each side, and ½-inch steaks 1 minute to a side. The meat should be served rare. Ed.

To serve 4:
    2 pounds boneless rib steaks
    6 tablespoons butter, in all
    2 medium-size onions, minced
    ⅓ cup red wine vinegar
    ½ cup Beaujolais Villages (or other light, dry red wine)
    ½ teaspoon peppercorns, slightly crushed
    Several sprigs fresh thyme (*or substitute ½ teaspoon dried thyme; Ed.*)
    1 rounded teaspoon tomato paste
    Coarse salt
    1 to 2 tablespoons peanut oil
    2 tablespoons mixed chopped fresh chervil, parsley, and tarragon (*use one or all, depending on seasonal availability; Ed.*)

PREPARATION OF THE SAUCE:

Melt 3 tablespoons of butter in a heavy 1-quart saucepan. Add the onions and cook them for 5 minutes over low heat, stirring frequently with a wooden spoon. The onions should be soft but not browned.

Add the vinegar to the onions and cook them over high heat until all the liquid has evaporated. Quickly add the wine, pepper, thyme, tomato paste, and a good pinch of coarse salt. Simmer the sauce gently over low heat for 20 minutes, or until only about 3 tablespoons of liquid remain. (*Press down on the onions when checking the quantity of liquid in the bottom of the saucepan. Ed.*)

Remove the sprigs of thyme, if fresh was used, and, stirring briskly, incorporate 2 tablespoons of butter a little at a time. Taste for seasoning. Cover the sauce and keep it warm, but do not let it heat beyond the barest simmer or the butter will separate.

COOKING THE MEAT:

Sprinkle the steaks lightly with salt and pepper. Melt 1 tablespoon of butter with as much oil as needed to coat a large heavy frying pan. When the butter sizzles and the oil begins to smoke, add the meat and cook it quickly for 10 seconds on each side.

If the frying pan is not large enough to cook all the steaks at once, either use two skillets or repeat the operation, keeping the cooked meat warm on a hot platter and adding more butter and oil to the skillet as necessary.

TO SERVE:

Spoon the hot onion sauce over the meat and sprinkle it with the chopped fresh herbs. Serve the *entrecôte* accompanied by Crisp Ruffled Potatoes (*pommes gaufrettes au beurre*, page 201).

Filet mignon de boeuf aux échalotes
FILET MIGNON WITH SHALLOTS
(Color picture 13)

To serve 4:
  1¾ pounds fillet of beef, completely trimmed
  Salt
  Freshly ground pepper
  2 ounces shallots (about 8)
  4 tablespoons butter, in all
  3 tablespoons red wine vinegar
  ¾ cup plus 1 tablespoon Concentrated Veal Stock with Tomato
    (*demi-glace tomatée*, page 17)
  ⅜ cup *crème fraîche* (page 22)

HAVE READY:

1. The *filet mignon*: Buy the meat from the tip of the fillet. Cut it into ¾-inch slices, and season well with salt and pepper.

2. The shallots: Peel them but be sure not to chop them until the last moment so that they will retain their freshness.

COOKING THE MEAT:

Choose a heavy skillet large enough to hold all the *filets mignons* easily, one next to the other. Heat 2 tablespoons of butter until sizzling and arrange the meat in the pan. Sear the *filets* for barely 2 minutes on each side.

Remove the *filets* and keep them warm on a hot plate inverted over a larger plate, so that the meat will not stew in its own juices. *(There will be a sufficient amount of juice rendered as the* filets *wait. Ed.)*

PREPARATION OF THE SAUCE:

Pour off the cooking butter from the skillet and reserve it for possible use with accompanying vegetables.

Deglaze the pan with vinegar and reduce it until completely evaporated. Add the *demi-glace*, then the *crème fraîche*, and bring to a boil over low heat. Simmer this sauce very gently until only ½ cup remains, then add the juices which have escaped from the cooked *filets*.

Take the skillet off the heat and whisk the remaining butter into the sauce. Taste for seasoning and return the *filets* to the pan. Carefully simmer them for 20 seconds without letting the sauce reach the boiling point.

TO SERVE:

At the last moment, coarsely chop the shallots. *(If they are cut any earlier they will become harsh and dry. Ed.)* Arrange the meat on a hot serving plate and sprinkle with the chopped shallots.

If they are in season, serve sautéed wild mushrooms as an accompaniment.

Boeuf cru sauce digoinaise
RAW BEEF WITH MUSTARD SAUCE

To serve 4:
    1¼ pounds boneless eye of the prime rib (*see Note*)
    2 cups watercress leaves, stems removed
    Coarse salt
    Mustard Sauce (*sauce digoinaise*, page 25)

NOTE: *This prime cut of beef is favored by the Japanese for many of their dishes. If you have difficulty in finding an accommodating butcher to cut the meat as required, an Oriental market might be helpful. Ed.*

    HAVE READY:

1. The beef: The meat for this recipe should be well aged and cut from the first rib into paper-thin slices.
    Trim the beef of all fat and arrange it on a chilled platter or individual plates.
2. The watercress: Wash and dry the leaves and arrange them harmoniously with the meat to create a sufficient contrast of color.

    TO SERVE:

Salt the beef lightly and run a thick ribbon of mustard sauce across the slices. Pass the remaining sauce separately.
    Serve this dish with firm brown bread, thinly sliced.

Jambon de Roanne enrubanné
HAM WITH VEGETABLE STREAMERS

This special ham of Roanne has been cooked in straw and "larded" with green peppercorns. However, the recipe may be prepared with *jambon d' York* or *jambon de Paris*.

To serve 4:
    4 thick slices *jambon de Roanne*, about 4 ounces each (*see Note*)
    10 tablespoons butter, in all
    Salt

Freshly ground pepper
½ lemon
2 whole cooked Vegetable Serpentines (*serpentins de légumes,* page 208)

NOTE: Jambon de Roanne *does not exist in the United States and the ham sometimes found labeled York ham is, most likely, not what you would find in France. For the purpose of this recipe, substitute either boiled ham or Virginia ham. If you use Virginia ham, make sure that all rind or other outside coating is removed, or its spicy sweetness will detract from the sauce. Ed.*

COOKING:

1. The ham: Melt 1½ to 2 tablespoons of butter in one or, if necessary, two large skillets. Lightly brown the ham on both sides, then arrange it on a hot platter.

2. The butter (*le beurre fondu*): In a small saucepan, bring 3 tablespoons of water to a boil over high heat. Using a wire whisk, incorporate the remaining butter, cut into tiny pieces, a little at a time. Stir briskly until thickened, then season with salt, pepper, and a few drops of lemon juice.

3. The vegetables: Cut the hot rolled vegetables into 12 coils each ½ inch thick.

TO SERVE:

Divide the ham slices among 4 hot plates. To decorate, arrange 3 coils over the center of each slice and unwind them slightly, so that they cover the entire plate harmoniously. Nap with the *beurre fondu.* (*This dish is most attractive presented on white plates. Ed.*)

Côtelettes de porc sauce confuse
PORK CHOPS WITH MINT, CITRUS, AND ONION SAUCE

To serve 4:

4 loin pork chops, about 8 ounces each, completely trimmed
Coarse salt
Freshly ground pepper
1 tomato
1 orange, preferably a navel orange
4 cloves garlic
3 tablespoons butter, in all
1 large onion, coarsely chopped
Juice of ½ lemon
8 mint leaves
1¼ cups Concentrated Veal Stock with Tomato (*demi-glace tomatée*, page 17)

HAVE READY:

1. The pork chops: When you have your butcher trim the chops, ask him to shorten the rib bone, cut off the backbone, and remove all fat. Sprinkle the chops with salt and pepper.

2. The tomato: Do not peel the tomato. Cut it into 8 wedges and remove the seeds.

3. The orange: Peel the orange close to the flesh, removing all white pith. Cut it into 4 round slices and, if it is not a navel orange, remove the seeds.

4. The garlic: Peel the garlic, cut it into thin slices lengthwise, and blanch them for 5 minutes in boiling water.

COOKING THE CHOPS:

Heat 2 tablespoons of butter in a large skillet. Arrange the chops, one next to the other, and sear them for 5 to 6 minutes on each side. Do not let them burn. Finish cooking the chops over low heat. Allow 15 minutes for this and turn them several times. When finished, set the chops aside on a hot serving platter, and place them in a very slow oven, or cover, to keep warm.

PREPARATION OF THE SAUCE:

Over medium to low heat, sauté the onion with the garlic in the remnants of cooking fat. Stir constantly until the onion becomes a rich dark brown, taking on color from the coagulated pan juices. Press down on the onion with a spoon and push it to one side of the skillet. Hold a small plate over the onion (to avoid losing it), and pour off all fat.

Return the skillet to the stove and deglaze with lemon juice. Add the mint leaves, tomato wedges, and orange slices. Pour the *demiglace* over all, and bring to a boil. Reduce the sauce to not quite ¾ cup, or just enough to coat the chops.

Taste for seasoning and stir in the remaining butter to give the sauce added gloss. Then, spoon the sauce over the pork chops and serve very hot.

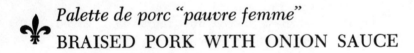

Palette de porc "pauvre femme"
BRAISED PORK WITH ONION SAUCE

To serve 4:
> One 2-pound pork shoulder roast with bone, or one 1½-pound
> boneless pork tenderloin with ½ pound additional bones
> 3 cloves garlic
> Salt
> Freshly ground pepper
> 7 tablespoons butter, in all
> 1¾ pounds onions (about 5 onions), thinly sliced
> 1 large potato, peeled and sliced
> *Bouquet garni* (sprigs of thyme and parsley and a bay leaf, tied
> together)
> 1 cup milk
> 2 tablespoons coarsely chopped parsley

PREPARE THE PORK:

Choose a pale piece of pork with a slightly rosy cast. Peel the garlic, and split each clove in two lengthwise. Make 6 small incisions around the meat and stuff each one with a piece of garlic. Season with salt and pepper.

COOKING:

Preheat oven to 325° F.

Melt 1½ tablespoons of butter in a casserole and, over medium to low heat, slowly brown the pork on all sides. Allow about 20 minutes for this operation.

At the same time, melt the remaining butter in a sauté pan, and cook the onions, turning them frequently, until soft and golden. Add the onions to the pork with the potato and *bouquet garni.*

Bring the milk to a boil and pour it over the meat. Cover the casserole and place it in the oven for 1 hour and 15 minutes. Baste and turn the meat several times during the cooking.

FINISHING THE SAUCE:

Remove the pork from the casserole and place it on a deep heatproof serving platter. Keep it warm in the turned-off oven.

Discard the *bouquet garni,* and pass the onions, potato, and cooking liquid through the fine blade of a food mill. You should obtain a sauce the consistency of a light purée. Skim off all surplus fat and taste for seasoning. Make sure that there is enough pepper.

TO SERVE:

Pour the sauce over the meat and simmer them together briefly (*see Note*).

Sprinkle the pork with parsley and serve it accompanied by Green Cabbage with Fresh Bacon (*chou vert au lardons,* page 187).

NOTE: *After simmering the pork in the sauce, I preferred to present it sliced, napped with a band of sauce and with parsley scattered over all. Ed.*

Le gibier

GAME

Lapin farci "Georgette Badaut"

RABBIT STUFFED WITH SPINACH AND MUSHROOMS

To serve 6:
    One 6-pound rabbit, about 4½ pounds dressed
    Salt
    Freshly ground pepper
    2 heaping tablespoons imported *moutarde blanche,* or substitute
        Dijon mustard
    3 shallots
    3½ tablespoons butter
    1 large branch fresh thyme
    2 cups *vin de Pommard* (or other dry red wine)
    1 cup *crème fraîche* (page 22), or heavy cream

    THE STUFFING (*la farce*):

    ¼ pound smoked bacon, in one piece
    ½ pound mushrooms, cooked
    ½ pound spinach, cooked
    2 shallots
    3 tablespoons butter
    1 teaspoon salt
    ½ teaspoon freshly ground pepper

PREPARATION OF THE FARCE:

1. Cut the bacon into a small dice and brown it lightly in a skillet over low heat.
2. Coarsely chop the mushrooms and spinach.
3. Finely chop the shallots and sauté them in 3 tablespoons of butter.
4. Combine the ingredients above in a bowl, add salt and pepper, and mix into a soft paste.

PREPARATION OF THE RABBIT:

1. Have your butcher prepare the rabbit in the following way: Cut off the front and hind feet below the joint and skin the rabbit. Save the head and ears, but remove the eyes. (*If this makes you uneasy, just don't bother with the head and ears. Ed.*)
2. Make a 4-inch slash through the skin of the chest cavity, where the ribs part, and extract the liver. Remove any filament and set the liver aside.

NOTE: *The 4-inch slash will not be necessary as, when one buys a rabbit in the United States, the entire body cavity has already been opened, not only in the area designated, but to a much larger extent. Ed.*

3. Lay the rabbit on its back and, using a spoon, fill the interior of the chest cavity with the *farce*.

Close the cavity with needle and thread. Then, turn the rabbit over onto its breast and tie the front legs to the shoulders in a crouching position, leaving the head resting in its natural way. Do the same with the hind legs.
4. Season the rabbit with salt and pepper and smear it all over with mustard.
5. Chop the shallots and liver. Set them aside.

COOKING:

Preheat oven to 500° F.

Melt the butter in a roasting pan (*not aluminum*) and roll the rabbit in it.

Place in the oven. After 10 minutes, lower the temperature to 400° F. Roast it 1 hour in all. Saturate a large branch of fresh thyme in ⅓ of the red wine (*see Note*) and use it to baste the rabbit frequently.

Remove the rabbit from the roasting pan, lay it on a hot platter, and cover to keep warm.

NOTE: *If a branch of fresh thyme is unavailable, sprinkle the rabbit lightly with dried thyme and use sprigs of parsley, tied together, as a basting brush. Ed.*

PREPARATION OF THE SAUCE:

Brown the shallots and liver in the roasting pan, then deglaze with the rest of the red wine, and reduce by half. Add the *crème fraîche* and boil the sauce gently until thickened.

TO SERVE:

Untruss the rabbit and pull out the thread used to secure the stuffing. Present the rabbit in its natural position, crouched on four legs. Coat with a little of the boiling sauce and serve the remainder in a hot sauceboat.

To carve: Divide the *farce* among 4 hot plates. Cut off the front shoulders and hind legs close to the body, then slice the saddle. Arrange the meat on the plates with the *farce* and nap with hot sauce.

Agates de palombes à la menthe
MORSELS OF PIGEON WRAPPED
IN MINT LEAVES

To serve 2 to 4:
    Cold butter, about 4 tablespoons
    2 pigeons (wood pigeons or wing doves), plucked, and cleaned
    1 shallot, finely chopped
    3½ ounces very lean salt pork (unsmoked bacon), diced
    1 tablespoon cognac
    ½ teaspoon peppercorns, crushed
    Coarse salt (*optional*)
    32 or 64 fresh mint leaves
    Sprigs of fresh thyme
    Sprigs of fresh rosemary
    1 small bay leaf
    Fresh Tomato Sauce (*coulis de tomates,* page 23)

HAVE READY:

1. The butter: With the help of a small tool, such as a melon-ball cutter, form 32 small balls of butter, each the size of a cherry pit.
2. The pigeons: Using a fillet knife, carefully carve out the breasts of the pigeons and remove the skin. With poultry shears, cut the carcasses into small pieces, and set them aside.
3. The shallot: Sauté the shallot in ½ tablespoon of butter, covered, for 5 minutes over low heat. Do not allow it to brown. Set aside.

PREPARATION:

Grind the salt pork in a meat grinder, followed by the pigeon fillets. Mix well with shallot, cognac, pepper, and, if the pork is not sufficiently salty, a dash of salt. We recommend that you try out a little piece in a skillet to be sure.

Cover each frozen stone of butter with approximately 2 teaspoons of the pigeon mixture. Roll them between your fingers, which have been moistened lightly with cognac. Wrap 1 or 2 mint leaves, depending on size, around each morsel, and lay them, side by side, on a steamer rack.

Spread the carcasses out over the bottom of the steamer or casserole, with the thyme, rosemary, and bay leaf. Add water until the carcasses are just covered. Make sure that the water level does not interfere with the steamer rack. Add the rack and cover the steamer tightly. Turn heat to high and, when the water begins to boil rapidly, steam for 5 minutes.

Take the rack from the heat and serve the *agates* immediately. You may serve this as an *hors d'oeuvre*, or as a first course, accompanied by Fresh Tomato Sauce.

NOTE: *Strain and save the flavorful broth for another use. Ed.*

Aiguillettes de "col vert" aux mousserons des près
SLICED MALLARD DUCK WITH WILD MUSHROOMS

To serve 4:
  2 wild mallard ducks, well hung
  1 tablespoon *foie gras*
  1 pound *mousserons* (*see Note*)
  Salt
  Freshly ground pepper
  3 tablespoons imported peanut oil
  3 tablespoons cognac
  4 shallots
  Bouquet garni (sprigs of thyme and parsley and a bay leaf, tied together)
  1⅔ cups Bourgogne (or other dry red Burgundy wine)
  1 cup Concentrated Veal Stock with Tomato (*demi-glace tomatée*, page 17), optional
  ⅝ cup *crème fraîche* (page 22)
  6 tablespoons butter
  1 tablespoon chopped parsley

168

HAVE READY:

1. The ducks: Choose young mallards, recognizable by the flexibility of the beak. Pluck, clean, and singe them, then cut off the part where the tail feathers were attached, and truss.

Reserve the livers, removing any green areas and filament. Pass them through a sieve, or food mill, with the *foie gras*, then refrigerate until needed.

2. The mushrooms (*mousserons*): Trim the mushrooms and rinse twice, without allowing them to soak. Cook the *mousserons* with a pinch of salt, covered, in their own juices for about 2 minutes.

NOTE: *Though* mousserons *may be found in the wild by experts, they are unavailable commercially in the United States. Substitute the most interesting mushrooms available, such as canned or dried* cèpes, chanterelles, *or morels. Ed.*

PREPARATION OF THE DUCKS:

Preheat oven to 475° F.

Season the ducks well with salt and pepper. Arrange them in a shallow roasting pan and brush lightly with peanut oil. Roast 20 minutes, turning on all sides.

It is preferable to cook the ducks 1 hour in advance. When precooked, the meat ceases to toughen and becomes a uniform rosy color.

After a short rest, untruss the ducks, and detach the leg-thigh sections. Following close to the breastbone, with a small sharp knife cut out the 2 whole breast fillets and then the tiny *filets mignons* attached to each carcass just below the breast. Separate the 4 wings at the joints. Cover the fillets and legs to keep warm.

PREPARATION OF THE SAUCE:

Using a meat cleaver, break up the necks, wings, and carcasses. Cook them in an ungreased, heavy casserole until well browned on all sides. Drain off the fat, if there is any, and deglaze the casserole with cognac.

Add 3 of the shallots, quartered, and the *bouquet garni*. Moisten with red wine and 1 cup of *demi-glace* or water. The bones should be totally covered by liquid. If not, add more *demi-glace* or water. Boil gently 1 hour, then strain through a fine sieve.

Rinse the casserole and return the broth to reduce further. Skim the surface frequently, and cook down to ⅝ cup.

Add *crème fraîche* and stir in the reserved liver purée to thicken the sauce. Taste for seasoning and correct, if necessary. When the sauce is ready, it must not boil again.

FINISHING THE DUCK AND THE MUSHROOMS:

Reheat the oven to 475° F.

Remove the skin from the large fillets (*optional*) and cut each one into 5 long thin slices. Leave the small fillets whole.

Drain the mushrooms and sauté them in butter for a few minutes, or until lightly browned. At the last moment, add the remaining shallot, chopped, and the parsley.

TO SERVE:

Mound the mushrooms in the center of a large hot platter. Surround them with a crown of sliced duck and the small fillets, overlapping slightly.

Arrange the legs in a pinwheel over the mushrooms and place the platter in the hot oven for 30 seconds. Then remove and pour a ribbon of sauce over the meat. Serve at once.

Pass the remaining sauce separately in a hot sauceboat.

Bécasse Maître Richard
WOODCOCK WITH RED WINE SAUCE

To serve 4:
    4 woodcocks (*see Note*)
    Coarse salt
    Freshly ground pepper
    6 tablespoons butter
    3 tablespoons *foie gras*
    4 thick slices white bread (slightly stale)
    3 tablespoons cognac
    ⅓ bottle (1 cup) Chambertin (or other robust red Burgundy)

½ cup Concentrated Veal Stock with Tomato (*demi-glace tomatée*, page 17)
2 zests of lemon
½ lemon

The duration of time for hanging woodcocks is regulated by the air temperature where they are being kept. In any case, do not exceed 8 days. The birds should be suspended by their feet.

NOTE: *If woodcock is not obtainable, snipe, which is closely related, can be substituted.*

Pigeon, though not the same (other than being a dark-meat bird), can be adapted to the recipe quite well, but in this case do not save the entrails, except for the heart and liver needed for the sauce. Instead, double the quantity of foie gras. Ed.

HAVE READY:

1. The woodcocks: Pluck the birds at the last moment, but do not clean them. Remove the eyes, then cross their legs, and secure them in place using the beak to hold them. There should not be any need to truss the birds. Season with salt and pepper. (*If you are substituting pigeons, return the hearts and livers to the breast cavity, and truss the birds. Ed.*)

COOKING:

Preheat oven to 475° F.
In a skillet just large enough to hold the birds side by side, heat the butter until it foams. Roll the woodcocks in the butter, then roast in the hot oven for 20 to 25 minutes. Take care to turn and baste them from time to time. Their meat should be pink, but not rare. When finished, do not turn off the oven.

PREPARATION OF THE *farce* AND THE CROÛTONS:

1. The *farce*: Using the back of a spoon, carefully extract the intestines of the woodcocks, taking care to remove and discard the gizzard. (The hard little ball is easily recognized.)
In a mortar or small mixing bowl, pound the entrails to a paste with the *foie gras*. Season the mixture with salt and pepper.
2. The toasts: Cut the bread into 4 rectangular croûtons 2 inches by 4 inches and ¾ inch thick. With a knife, draw a rectangle within,

1½ inches by 3 inches, then brown them under the broiler. (*This should only take a minute. Watch carefully that they do not burn. Ed.*)

Using the point of a knife, detach the lid of each croûton within its boundaries, making 4 small boxes. Fill each of them with half the *farce*.

PREPARATION OF THE SAUCE:

After roasting the woodcocks, pour off the cooking juices and reserve them in a small bowl. Deglaze the skillet with cognac, then add the wine, *demi-glace*, and lemon zest. Boil down until greatly reduced, then add the reserved juices with a squeeze of lemon.

Return the sauce to a boil and incorporate the remainder of the *farce* until thickened. Taste for seasoning.

FINISHING THE WOODCOCKS:

Split the birds in half and remove the breastbone. (*I prefer to cut out the backbone too, using poultry shears. Ed.*) Simmer them in hot sauce for 2 minutes.

Meanwhile heat the croûtons in the oven, then arrange the birds on top. Pass the sauce separately in a hot sauceboat. Serve the opened bottle of Chambertin with the woodcocks.

Compote de lapin de garenne aux abricots secs
RABBIT WITH APRICOTS IN RED WINE SAUCE

To serve 4:
    1 young domestic rabbit, about 4½ pounds dressed
    1 cup red Burgundy
    ⅜ cup red wine vinegar
    2 cloves garlic, unpeeled
    Bouquet garni (sprigs of thyme and parsley and a bay leaf, tied
        together)
    5 ounces finest-quality dried apricots
    Coarse salt
    Freshly ground pepper
    3 tablespoons imported peanut oil
    4 tablespoons butter, in all

1. The rabbit: Skin and clean the rabbit according to directions on page 165. Reserve the liver, removing any filament.

Bone the saddle, legs, and shoulders, and cut the meat into cubes, weighing about 1 ounce each. Marinate the meat in the wine and vinegar with the garlic and *bouquet garni* for 12 hours.

2. The dried apricots: Cut the apricots in half, if they are large, and soak them in cold water for 1 hour.

COOKING:

Drain the rabbit, reserving the *garniture* and marinade. Dry the meat well with a towel, then season with salt and pepper. *(The rabbit must be dried thoroughly, or it will not brown properly. Ed.)*

Heat the oil with 2 tablespoons of butter in a large heavy casserole. Add the rabbit and brown it on all sides. Then, add the garlic (*see Note*) and *bouquet garni*, cover the casserole, and let the rabbit and *garniture* stew together for 20 minutes over low heat. Meanwhile, drain the apricots.

Off heat, add the reserved marinade and apricots to the rabbit. Then, stirring, bring the liquid to a simmer. Cut a circle of wax paper the diameter of the casserole, butter it lightly, and place over the rabbit. Re-cover the casserole and simmer 20 minutes. Midway through the cooking, add the reserved liver, quartered.

NOTE: *Tie the garlic in a thin piece of cheesecloth and attach the string to the handle of the casserole. This way it can be easily extracted when you need it. Ed.*

FINISHING THE SAUCE:

Retrieve the cloves of garlic and remove the peel. Mash the garlic into a paste with the remaining 2 tablespoons of butter.

Using a slotted spoon or skimmer, remove the rabbit and apricots, temporarily, from the sauce. Discard the *bouquet garni*.

Then stir the garlic butter into the sauce, a little at a time. When the butter is evenly distributed, return the rabbit and apricots to the sauce, and taste for seasoning.

TO SERVE:

Alternate the morsels of rabbit with the apricots on a deep round platter. Spoon the sauce over all and serve. *(This dish will not suffer being reheated. Ed.)*

Daube de lièvre au vin d'Ambierle
HARE IN RED WINE

To serve 5 to 6:

>One 5- to 6-pound hare, about 4 pounds dressed (*see Note*)
>3½ to 4 cups *vin d'Ambierle*, a dry red wine from Roanne (or other dry red wine)
>5 cloves garlic, peeled
>2 bay leaves
>4 fresh mint leaves
>1 basil leaf
>1 branch thyme (*or substitute ½ teaspoon dried thyme; Ed.*)
>2 rounded teaspoons tomato paste
>½ teaspoon coriander seeds, crushed
>½ teaspoon peppercorns, crushed
>2 large strips orange peel, zest only
>2 large strips lemon peel, zest only
>Coarse salt
>4 ounces very lean salt pork (unsmoked bacon), in one piece

NOTE: *A rabbit may be substituted for the hare, in which case add the salt pork after 2 hours, and decrease the cooking time to 3 hours in all. Ed.*

HAVE READY:

(The evening before)

1. The hare: Choose a hare called *trois quarts* (three-quarters), so named because it is the firstborn of the season. In order to recognize it, check the weight which must be between 5 and 6 pounds and, in any case, should not exceed 6 pounds.

Skin and clean the hare, reserving the blood and liver, separately, for the sauce. Remove any filament from the liver. (*The only way you can expect to collect the blood is to be present when the hare is killed. Since this may be unlikely, don't be concerned. However, if it is possible, then add a drop or two of vinegar to the blood to prevent it from coagulating. Ed.*)

Cut the hare into 18 pieces: Eight from the hind legs, 4 from the shoulder, and 6 pieces from the loin and breast. Place them in a medium-size enameled cast-iron casserole, and add the marinade of aromatic herbs, garlic, tomato paste, coriander, pepper, and enough red wine to cover completely. Refrigerate the rabbit overnight.

(The next day)

2. The zests: Chop the zests coarsely, place them in a small sauce-pan, and cover with cold water. Bring to a boil, blanch 1 minute, then drain in a sieve. Add to the marinade.

3. The salt pork: Remove the skin from the salt pork and chop it into tiny pieces. Cut the meat into thick *lardons* 1½ inches long and ¼ inch wide. Put them in a saucepan, cover with cold water, bring to a boil, and blanch 2 minutes. Drain and set aside.

4. The liver: Slice the liver into 4 small scallops and reserve them in the refrigerator.

COOKING:

Take the cold casserole from the refrigerator and place it on the stove. Add the zests and sprinkle lightly with coarse salt. Over moderate heat, bring the marinade to a gentle boil. As soon as you hear the sound of a simmer, turn the heat to very low and, without lifting the lid, cook the hare 3 hours.

After 3 hours, add the *lardons* with the chopped rind, and cook, over lowest possible heat, 2 hours longer.

Five minutes before the hare is done, use a large spoon to skim off all fat and any bay leaves and herbs that may have floated to the surface.

NOTE: *At this time, if you feel the liquid in the casserole seems too thin, remove the rabbit, and boil down the sauce until reduced by about half. Then, return the rabbit and proceed. Ed.*

Add the slices of liver, and the blood, if possible. Barely simmer the *daube* for 5 minutes, then taste for seasoning.

TO SERVE:

Serve the *daube* from the same casserole in which it was cooked, ac-companied by Pasta Shells with Truffles (*coquillettes aux truffes "Jolly Martine,"* page 210).

NOTE: *I found this dish most satisfactory reheated the next day. It could be an idea to plan a span of 3 days from marinating to serving. Ed.*

Perdreaux aux lentilles vertes
PARTRIDGES WITH GREEN LENTILS

To serve 4:

½ cup green lentils from Puy (*or substitute regular lentils; Ed.*)

1 carrot

1 onion

Bouquet garni (sprigs of thyme and parsley and a bay leaf, tied together)

Coarse salt

4 young partridges, about 12 ounces each

10 tablespoons butter, in all

Freshly ground pepper

1½ tablespoons cognac

1 tablespoon *foie gras*

1 rounded teaspoon imported *moutarde blanche forte*, or substitute Dijon mustard

1 onion, finely chopped

⅜ cup red wine

HAVE READY:

1. The lentils: The evening before, soak the lentils in cold water. (*A long period of soaking is not usually as necessary with lentils as it is with beans. Several hours will be sufficient. Ed.*)

The next day, drain the lentils and put them in a casserole with 4 times their volume of water (2 cups). Bring almost to a boil and remove the scum which forms on the surface. Then add the carrot, onion, *bouquet garni*, and salt. Reduce the heat to a simmer, and cook about 30 minutes, or until just tender. Check frequently to see if they are done.

2. The partridges: They must be hung, but though you do not want them freshly killed, you do not want them gamy either. (*Between 5 and 7 days is sufficient. Ed.*)

Pluck, clean, and singe them. Reserve the livers, removing any green spots and filament. Cut off the feet and the necks close to the body, but be sure to pull back the skin of the neck to provide enough covering for the vent when the birds are trussed.

Rub the inside of each partridge with a pinch of coarse salt, then deposit ½ tablespoon of butter within. Truss them, resting the legs against each side of the breast.

3. Prepare the *liaison*: Season the livers with salt and pepper. Heat 2 tablespoons of butter in a small skillet and quickly brown them in it. Allow no more than 1 minute for this, then deglaze the pan with cognac.

Pass the livers, cooking butter, cognac, *foie gras*, and mustard through a fine sieve into a small bowl. Set the purée aside.

COOKING:

Preheat oven to 475° F.

Heat 4 tablespoons of butter in a heavy skillet or roasting pan. Roll the partridges in the butter, then place in the oven for 25 minutes. Turn and baste them 3 times while they are roasting. When finished, let the partridges rest at room temperature in a warm place. (*Do not turn off the oven. Ed.*)

Heat the remaining 2 tablespoons of butter in a medium-size casserole and sauté the chopped onion over medium heat. Stir frequently until golden, then deglaze the casserole with red wine, and reduce until the liquid has evaporated completely. Add the lentils, drained of all but a small amount of their cooking liquid. Discard the other vegetables and the *bouquet garni*.

FINISHING THE LENTILS AND THE PARTRIDGES:

Add the liver *liaison* to the lentils. Stir well and taste for seasoning.

Warm the partridges 2 to 3 minutes in the hot oven, then untruss.

Make a bed of the lentils on a deep hot serving platter and rest the birds on top. Pass the remnants of cooking butter from the roasting pan separately, in a very hot sauceboat.

Sarcelles aux pêches
TEAL WITH PEACHES

NOTE: *Teal* (sarcelle) *is a freshwater duck, not unlike a mallard, though much smaller in size. If you use larger ducks, allow for additional cooking time. Ed.*

To serve 4:
    4 teal that have been hung
    Salt
    Freshly ground pepper
    Imported peanut oil
    4 yellow peaches
    1¼ cups sugar
    1 tablespoon cognac
    1 tablespoon apricot jam
    3 tablespoons red wine vinegar
    Juice of ½ lemon
    1 cup Concentrated Veal Stock with Tomato (*demi-glace tomatée,*
        page 17)
    6 tablespoons butter
    Powdered sugar

HAVE READY:

1. The teal: Pluck and clean the birds. Cut off the part where the tail feathers were attached, then singe and truss them. Season with salt and pepper and brush with a little peanut oil.

2. The peaches: If they are very ripe, their skins will pull off easily. If not, plunge them into boiling water for 1 minute, then peel. Bring 3 cups of water to a boil with 1¼ cups of sugar. Split the peaches in half, remove the pits, and poach the halves 5 minutes in the sugar syrup. Let the peaches remain in the syrup until it is time to finish them.

COOKING THE DUCKS:

Preheat oven to 475° F.

Place the teal in a cast-iron roasting pan or skillet. Roast about 12 minutes, turning them on all sides. Remove from the oven and let stand in a warm place for ½ hour. (*If you are roasting small mallard ducks, allow 20 minutes. Cook longer if they are large. Ed.*)

178

THE SAUCE:

Pour off all fat from the roasting pan and deglaze with cognac. Add apricot jam and vinegar, and cook until caramelized, then add the juice of half a lemon, followed by the *demi-glace*. Reduce for 5 minutes over high heat. During this time, carefully skim the surface of any impurities.

Pass the sauce through a fine sieve and, over low heat, whisk in the butter, cut into tiny pieces, a little at a time. The sauce should achieve a glossy brilliance. Taste for seasoning.

FINISHING THE PEACHES:

Preheat the broiler.

Drain the peach halves and place them on a baking sheet. Sprinkle with powdered sugar, then pass them under the broiler to reheat and brown slightly.

TO SERVE:

Untruss the ducks. *(If using larger birds, split or quarter them. Ed.)* Place them in the center of a hot platter, nap with sauce, and surround with peach halves.

Selle de chevreuil panée au poivre blanc
SADDLE OF VENISON WITH WHITE PEPPERCORNS

(Color picture 12)

To serve 4:
- 1 saddle of venison, about 2½ pounds
- 2 tablespoons virgin olive oil
- 1 tablespoon white peppercorns
- 3 tablespoons butter
- 2 tablespoons cognac
- ½ cup dry white wine
- ½ cup Game Stock (*fond de gibier*, page 19)
- ⅝ cup *crème fraîche* (page 22), or heavy cream

PREPARATION OF THE VENISON:

The saddle is comprised of the first loin chops after the legs. Using a narrow sharp knife, remove the skin covering the meat, then roll the saddle in olive oil.

Crush the peppercorns coarsely with a rolling pin (*or with a mortar and pestle; Ed.*), then coat the venison on all sides with them. Press in so the meat is evenly encrusted with the pepper. Refrigerate overnight.

COOKING:

Preheat oven to 475° F.

Melt the butter in a heavy roasting pan. *(Do not use aluminum. Ed.)* Place the meat in it and roast 35 to 40 minutes, basting frequently.

Remove the venison and keep it warm on a hot platter, with a piece of buttered wax paper.

PREPARATION OF THE SAUCE:

Pour off all cooking fat from the roasting pan, then deglaze with cognac. Add the white wine and cook until reduced by half. Then add the game stock. (This could be replaced by good veal juices.) Bring to a boil, add the *crème fraîche*, and reduce until thickened.

Taste for seasoning. Do not forget to add the juices rendered while the meat rested. Remember *not* to add pepper.

CARVING:

Remove the 2 large fillets, cutting close to the bone, and slice them into 12 medallions. Then, take out the 2 *filets mignons* found on the inside of the saddle and cut them into 8 thin scallops.

TO SERVE:

Arrange the medallions in a crown on a hot serving platter and fill the interior with the carved *filets mignons*.

Nap with boiling sauce and any grains of pepper that have detached themselves during the carving. Serve with Chestnut Soufflé (*marrons en soufflé*, page 198).

Côtes de marcassin "Fructidor"
YOUNG WILD BOAR WITH FRUIT GARNITURE

To serve 4:

    8 chops of young wild boar taken from the loin, about 3½ pounds
        trimmed (*see Note*)
    2 tablespoons peanut oil
    1 small onion, sliced
    1 small carrot, sliced
    4 small semi-ripe pears, about 1¼ pounds
    2½ teaspoons sugar, in all
    12 tablespoons butter, in all
    4 small, tart green apples
    8 large chestnuts (*allow a few extra to have in reserve; Ed.*)
    4 large prunes (*or 8 if they are small; Ed.*)
    Coarse salt
    Freshly ground pepper
    2 shallots, chopped
    ¼ cup red wine vinegar
    ⅓ cup dry white wine
    12 juniper berries, slightly crushed

NOTE: *If young wild boar is unavailable, purchase a loin of pork. It will be about the same size and perfectly adaptable to this recipe. Treat the pork, in every respect, as directed for wild boar. However, with your purchase, include a pork shank to enrich the sauce. Ed.*

    HAVE READY:

    1. The wild boar (*le marcassin*): A young wild boar should weigh between 60 and 80 pounds. Have your butcher cut 8 chops from the loin, removing all superficial fat, and the backbone. Leave only the rib. Then ask him to flatten them slightly with the side of a meat cleaver. Save every bit of backbone, cut into manageable pieces, and all trimmings except fat.

NOTE: *If you are substituting loin of pork, bone the additional shank, and cut its meat and skin into manageable pieces. Use these and the stripped bone as a replacement for the wild-boar trimmings. Ed.*

2. The stock: Place the bones and trimmings in a casserole with a little oil and brown them on all sides. As soon as the meat begins to color nicely, add the onion and carrot. After a few minutes, moisten with 2 cups of water, and bring to a gentle boil. Cook the stock 1 hour, partially covered. Stir the bones and vegetables occasionally, and add more water from time to time to compensate for evaporation.

Pour the stock through a sieve and discard the bones and vegetables. Skim off all fat from the surface, then return the stock to a clean heavy saucepan. Boil until reduced to ⅝ cup.

PREPARATION OF THE FRUITS:

(All fruits should be cooked as near to the time of the cooking of the chops as possible, so that they will be warm when they are served. However, if necessary, they may be gently reheated. Ed.)

1. The pears: The pears should be slightly underripe in order to hold their shape. Quarter and peel them, and remove their cores and seeds. Trim the 16 quarters into neat, even shapes and, before they have a chance to discolor, drop them into a medium-size casserole with 1 cup of water, 2 tablespoons of butter, and 1 teaspoon of sugar.

Gently boil the pears, uncovered, until all liquid has evaporated, and the pears are golden and lightly caramelized. Adjust the heat so as not to overcook. *(Allow about 20 minutes cooking time and, when done, cover to keep warm. Ed.)*

2. The apples: Prepare the apples exactly as for the pears, though the cooking times of both fruits will depend upon their degree of ripeness.

3. The chestnuts: Cut a notch in each shell and drop the chestnuts into boiling water. Cook 5 minutes, then drain and peel them.

Place the chestnuts in a small saucepan just large enough to hold them, and add 1½ tablespoons of butter and ½ teaspoon of sugar. Cover the saucepan and cook 20 minutes over low heat, stirring frequently.

4. The prunes: Soak them overnight in enough cold water to cover. The next day, bring to a boil in the same water. At the first sign of a simmer, remove from heat, and drain immediately. Cut the prunes in half and extract the pits.

Just before serving, sauté the prunes briefly in 1½ tablespoons butter.

COOKING THE CHOPS:

Melt 3 tablespoons of butter in a heavy skillet. Season the chops liberally on both sides with salt and pepper, and arrange them side by side in the pan. To make sure that they do not become dry, brown them slowly over medium heat, turning to brown both sides. Then, lower the heat, cover, and cook about 20 minutes. Turn the chops midway through the cooking.

When they are done, arrange the chops on a hot platter and cover to keep warm.

PREPARATION OF THE SAUCE:

Drain all fat from the skillet used to cook the meat, leaving only the residue of dark natural juices. Add the shallots to the pan and cook 20 seconds.

Deglaze the skillet with vinegar, then add the white wine. Reduce slightly, and add the stock and juniper berries. Boil the sauce gently until reduced to ½ cup.

Whisk in the remaining 2 tablespoons of butter, cut into tiny pieces, to give the sauce gloss. Taste for seasoning. When it is finished, the sauce must not boil again.

TO SERVE:

Place the chops in the center of a hot serving platter. Arrange the cooked fruits harmoniously around them, alternating their colors.

Spoon the hot sauce over the chops and serve at once.

Les légumes & les pâtes

VEGETABLES & PASTA

Cuisson des légumes verts
COOKING GREEN VEGETABLES

Use the following rules for cooking string beans, peas, spinach, and asparagus tips successfully. Be forewarned, these vegetables must be crisp to the bite. Prolonged cooking takes away their taste, color, and shape.

1. Use a "stainless" cooking utensil such as one made of stainless steel, or copper lined with stainless steel but not with tin.

2. Plunge the vegetables into large quantities of rapidly boiling, salted water. Allow 2 teaspoons of salt to each quart of water. Do not cover.

3. Keep the water at a rolling boil throughout the cooking.

4. When the proper degree of doneness has been achieved, drain the vegetables, season them, and serve immediately

If vegetables must wait, which is often the case, drain any of them, except asparagus, at the point of doneness, and quickly place them under cold running water; or better yet, plunge them into a basin of ice water. As soon as they are chilled, drain again, and keep the vegetables cool until ready to use.

To serve *à l'anglaise*, drop them once more into boiling water for only as long as it takes to get them hot. Drain, season, and serve them at once.

Cuisson des asperges
COOKING ASPARAGUS

Allow about 1 pound of asparagus per person.

Cooking asparagus is simple if one observes three rules:

1. Choose asparagus as fresh as possible. One can recognize their freshness at the point where they have been cut. *(When preparing asparagus, I find it advisable to remove the tough ends of the stalks by breaking them off where they tend to snap most easily. Ed.)*

2. Peel the lower part of each stalk with a vegetable peeler. Also remove any small leaves that may appear farther up the stalk. Wash the asparagus and tie them in small bundles of 8 to 10, then trim them to a uniform length of about 8 inches.

3. Overcooked asparagus loses its flavor; 6 to 10 minutes of cooking, depending on size, should be sufficient. Cook the asparagus in the classic manner—that is to say, drop the bundles into rapidly boiling, salted water. Contrary to the method of cooking other green vegetables, one does not usually refresh asparagus with cold water when they are done.

Aubergines Stendhal
EGGPLANT STUFFED WITH TOMATOES

To serve 6:

4 long eggplants, about 6 ounces each
Salt
Freshly ground pepper
1 pound tomatoes *(see Note)*
12 tablespoons butter, in all
1 whole head garlic, unpeeled
4 large fresh basil leaves

NOTE: *This dish may be served hot or cold. However, if you plan to serve it cold, be sure to see the changes in the ingredients described at the end of the recipe. Ed.*

HAVE READY:

1. The eggplants: Choose eggplants of equal size, freshly picked, and with a glossy deep-violet skin. Wipe them and cut off each end. Using a large knife, make 4 slashes, lengthwise, three-quarters of the way through each eggplant.

Arrange them on a plate and sprinkle lightly with salt and pepper. Let the eggplants stand at least 15 minutes to release some of their moisture.

2. The tomatoes: After trimming the stem end, cut the tomatoes in half crosswise. Place them on your work surface, cut side down, and slice into pieces about ½ inch thick. There should be about 32 half-slices in all.

NOTE: *In season, 2 large beefsteak tomatoes are perfect for this recipe. A half-slice will completely fill each of the slashes made in the egg-plants, in which case 16 pieces of tomato should be sufficient. Ed.*

PREPARATION:

Season the tomato slices with salt and pepper, and stick them from end to end in the slashes in the eggplants. *(Use 4 to 8 half-slices for each eggplant, depending on size. Ed.)*

Tie the eggplants tightly with string to preserve their shape and to hold the tomatoes in place.

COOKING:

Lay the eggplants, cut side up and side by side, in a casserole just large enough to accommodate them.

Dissolve 1 teaspoon of salt in 3 cups of cold water, and pour it over the eggplants. Add the butter, cut into small pieces, and the whole head of garlic. Cover the casserole and begin to cook the eggplants over medium to high heat. As soon as the water reaches the boiling point, reduce heat to a simmer, and cook 30 to 45 minutes, depending on the size of the eggplant.

Using a large fork or a skimmer, remove the eggplants, suspending them for a moment to drain. Then place them on a heatproof serving platter.

FINISHING THE EGGPLANT:

Over high heat, reduce the cooking liquid until only ½ cup of syrupy juice remains. Strain through a fine sieve, pressing down on the garlic, then pour the juice over the eggplant. Remove the string from the eggplant and baste with the juice. Simmer a few minutes, then sprinkle with freshly chopped basil. Serve very hot.

A COLD VARIATION OF THIS RECIPE:

Replace the butter with ¾ cup olive oil. Add the juice of ½ lemon and a *bouquet garni.*

After cooking, reduce the liquid remaining in the casserole to 6 tablespoons. Strain, and pour it over the eggplant. When the dish has cooled, refrigerate overnight. Serve the eggplant the next day, at room temperature.

Chou vert aux lardons
GREEN CABBAGE WITH FRESH BACON

To serve 4:
   1 green cabbage, about 2¼ pounds
   Salt
   6 ounces lean salt pork (unsmoked bacon), in one piece
   1 tablespoon peanut oil
   ¼ cup red wine vinegar
   6 tablespoons butter
   Freshly ground pepper, preferably white

HAVE READY:

1. The cabbage: Choose a large green cabbage or, out of season, a curly Savoy cabbage. Separate all the leaves, discarding the large ones from the exterior, and trim the core wherever it is predominant.

Wash the leaves and drop them into a large kettle of boiling salted water. Blanch 10 minutes, then drain. Rinse the leaves in cold water and drain again. Spread them out on a worktable and chop coarsely, lengthwise and crosswise, to make them more manageable.

2. The salt pork: Cut the salt pork into *lardons* 2½ inches long and ½ inch thick. Blanch them in boiling water for 2 to 3 minutes, then drain in a sieve.

COOKING:

Put the drained *lardons* in a saucepan with the peanut oil, and brown them in this and their own fat, on all sides, over low heat. Drain on paper towels and set aside.

Preheat oven to 400° F.

Put the cabbage in a large heavy casserole, moisten it with ⅓ cup of water, and season lightly with salt—depending on the saltiness of the *lardons*. Cut a circle of wax paper to fit the casserole, oil lightly, and lay it over the cabbage. Cover the casserole and place in the oven for 25 minutes.

FINISHING THE CABBAGE:

Remove the cover and the wax paper from the casserole and make sure that no liquid remains.

In a small heavy saucepan, bring the vinegar to a boil, reduce by half, then stir in the butter, cut into tiny pieces, a little at a time. When a *liaison* has formed, pour it over the cabbage, and toss gently with two wooden spoons. Add the *lardons*, cover the casserole, and simmer 5 minutes.

Serve the cabbage on a hot platter with a generous sprinkling of pepper.

Côtes de blettes à la fourme de Montbrison
SWISS CHARD IN CHEESE SAUCE

To serve 4 to 6:
    2 pounds Swiss chard
    2 egg yolks
    1¼ cups *crème fraîche* (page 22)
    3½ tablespoons butter
    3 ounces *fourme de Montbrison* (see Note)
    Coarse salt
    Freshly ground pepper, preferably white

NOTE: Fourme de Montbrison *is one of many French cheeses that do not meet the pasteurization requirements necessary for importation into the United States. Two suitable French cheeses to use as substitutes are* fourme d'Ambert *and* Saint-Gorlon. *English Stilton may also be used. Ed.*

PREPARE THE SWISS CHARD:

Choose the chards freshly cut, with large, clean white stems. Strip off the green part of the leaves and save only the stems. (*Cook the greens separately on another occasion. Ed.*) Remove the strings from the stems and the transparent skin, as you would clean a stalk of celery but more thoroughly. Cut the stems into pieces approximately 2 inches long and 1 inch wide. Wash and drain.

COOKING:

In a small bowl, mix together 2 egg yolks and 1 tablespoon of *crème fraîche*.

Melt the butter in a casserole, add the Swiss chard stems, and cook, covered, for 15 minutes over low heat. Stir frequently and do not allow the stems to brown. Add the remaining *crème fraîche* to the casserole (but not yet the egg-yolk *liaison*) and finish cooking the chard, covered, for about 10 minutes over low heat. Stir occasionally and check for doneness. The stems should be tender, yet remain crisp.

In a small heavy saucepan, melt the cheese over low heat. Warm it just long enough so that you can mash it to a paste, then blend it into the Swiss chard.

FINISHING THE SWISS CHARD:

Preheat the broiler.

Over the lowest heat possible, incorporate the egg-yolk *liaison* into the Swiss chard. Mix thoroughly and do not allow it to boil. Add salt and a generous amount of coarsely ground pepper.

Using two wooden spoons, lift the stems out of the sauce and layer them, lengthwise, in a lightly buttered 12-inch oval *au gratin* dish.

Stirring continuously, carefully heat the sauce remaining in the casserole a little longer, until slightly thickened. Then pour it over the Swiss chard and *gratiné* briefly under the broiler. When the sauce is lightly browned, serve at once.

Duo de truffes à la vapeur
STEAMED TRUFFLES WITH POTATOES

To serve 4:
 5½ to 6 ounces fresh, uncooked truffles (*see Note*)
 ½ pound new potatoes
 Salt
 Freshly ground pepper
 Coarse salt
 Cold butter

To prepare this recipe, it is imperative that you have a potato or vegetable steamer, or else use a grill on a trivet set in a casserole with a lid.

NOTE: *This recipe was created especially for fresh truffles. Though one can improvise with preserved truffles, it will not be the same. Ed.*

HAVE READY:

1. The truffles: Make sure they are very clean; if they are not, brush them under running water.

2. The potatoes: Cut them into the same number of pieces as you have truffles. Then trim the pieces into the same shape and size as the truffles.

COOKING:

Fill the steamer with water, just to the height of the grill.

Season the potatoes and truffles with salt and pepper and arrange them on the grill. Cover, and bring the water to a boil. Reduce the heat immediately to a simmer, and steam 25 minutes.

TO SERVE:

Cut the potato balls and the truffles into 2 or 3 slices each, and divide them among 4 hot plates. Sprinkle with coarse salt and pass the butter separately so that the guests may serve themselves to their own taste.

Should you prefer to eliminate the potatoes, we advise that you steam the truffle over a mixture of half (sweet) Sauternes and half dry white wine; this will enhance their perfume. When the truffles are cooked, bring the wine back to a boil and stir in butter, cut into tiny pieces, until a *liaison* is formed. Pour this sauce over the truffles and serve at once.

Émin021c121 d'artichaut au cerfeuil ⚜
BRAISED ARTICHOKE BOTTOMS
WITH CHERVIL

To serve 4:
  6 medium-size artichokes
  1 lemon
  ½ cup distilled white vinegar
  2 tablespoons butter
  1 large shallot, chopped
  3 tablespoons dry white wine
  Salt

Freshly ground pepper
¾ cup *crème fraîche* (page 22)
1 rounded teaspoon Dijon mustard
2 tablespoons chopped fresh chervil (*or substitute parsley; Ed.*)

PREPARATION OF THE ARTICHOKES:

Choose artichokes as freshly picked as possible. (*Select those with leaves tightly closed; Ed.*) Cut or break off the stems close to the bottoms, and tear off two or more layers of tough outside leaves. Trim the tops down to 1 inch above their bases and, using a small sharp knife, trim the bottoms neatly. As you do so, rub each artichoke well with half a lemon. Plunge them immediately into a bowl of cold water to which vinegar has been added to prevent them from darkening.

Take the artichokes from the water one at a time, cut them into quarters, and pull out the chokes. Rub each one again with lemon, and return them to the acidulated water. Do not drain the artichokes until just before you are ready to cook them.

COOKING:

Melt the butter over low heat in a heavy casserole just large enough to hold the artichokes side by side. Add the shallot and cook, covered, over low heat until soft. Do not allow it to brown.

Deglaze the pan with white wine and arrange the artichokes inside. Add enough water to cover them halfway. Season them liberally with salt and pepper, and bring the liquid to a boil. Cover the casserole tightly and adjust heat to a simmer. Cook the artichokes 35 minutes. (*At this point, you can remove the artichokes from the heat, keeping them warm, covered, until time to complete their cooking. Ed.*)

FINISHING THE ARTICHOKES:

Remove the cover from the casserole, raise the heat, and let the liquid reduce to about 2 tablespoons. Remove the artichokes and keep them warm.

Add the *crème fraîche* to the casserole, bring to a boil, then reduce the heat slightly, and simmer a few minutes. Stir in the mustard, taste for seasoning, and return the artichokes to the casserole. Simmer 5 minutes, basting continuously with the sauce.

Serve the artichokes in deep plates, liberally sprinkled with chervil.

Frison de concombres

JULIENNE OF CUCUMBERS IN CREAM

To serve 4:
  2 large cucumbers, about 1½ pounds
  1½ cups heavy cream (*see Note*)
  Coarse salt
  Freshly ground pepper, preferably white
  ½ lemon

PREPARE THE CUCUMBERS:

Choose freshly picked cucumbers. (*If they are small, use 3 or 4. Ed.*) Cut the ends off and divide them into pieces 3 to 4 inches long. Peel the pieces and cut them in half lengthwise. Remove the seeds, then cut the flesh into very thin *julienne* strips. Firm them in ice water for about 12 hours, changing the water 2 or 3 times.

When ready to proceed, drain the cucumbers and dry them well in a towel.

COOKING:

Pour the heavy cream into a medium-size casserole, add salt, and bring it to a boil. Reduce by half, or until very thick.

NOTE: *The Troisgros recipe called for ¾ cup* crème fraîche *boiled until reduced. In trying this, I found that the improvised* crème fraîche *(page 22) tends to curdle before it becomes thick enough to withstand the added moisture from the cucumbers. I found it very satisfactory to start instead with twice the amount of heavy cream, and to reduce it until very thick, with no problem of curdling. Ed.*

Add the cucumbers. They will release water and thin the cream. Boil for 5 minutes, allowing the sauce to rebuild its consistency. Add a generous grinding of pepper and a squeeze of lemon juice. Taste for seasoning. It will probably need a little more salt.

Serve the cucumbers in individual ramekins as an accompaniment to fish or white meats.

⚜ *Haricots blancs au vin rouge*
WHITE BEANS IN RED WINE SAUCE

To serve 4:

1½ pounds fresh white beans, unshelled (*see Note*)
Salt
1 onion, stuck with 1 clove
1 small carrot
Bouquet garni (sprigs of thyme and parsley and a bay leaf, tied
together)
5 tablespoons butter, in all
3 shallots, chopped
¾ cup red wine
1 clove garlic, chopped
Freshly ground pepper
2 tablespoons chopped parsley

NOTE: You can prepare this recipe with dried beans. Soak them for 2 hours in warm water before cooking, then bring to a boil and skim the surface. Simmer the beans about 1 hour or until tender.

COOKING:

Shell the beans at the last moment, and if they have an exterior skin, remove it. Drop them into a kettle of boiling salted water (1½ teaspoons salt to each quart water) and, using a cooking spoon, remove the scum as it rises to the surface.

Then, add the onion, carrot, and *bouquet garni*. Cook about 30 minutes, depending on the variety of white beans being used.

In a heavy casserole, sauté the shallots in 2½ tablespoons of butter, covered, for 2 minutes over low heat. Then add the red wine, bring to a boil, and cook until the bottom of the casserole is nearly dry.

Add the beans, partially drained, to the wine-shallot reduction. Reserve the remainder of their cooking liquid. Stir in the garlic and simmer the beans 10 minutes. Add pepper and taste for seasoning.

FINISHING THE BEANS:

Cut the remaining butter into pieces the size of hazelnuts and stir them, one by one, into the beans. Gently sauté the beans until the butter is distributed enough to form a *liaison*. The beans should bathe lightly in broth; if not, add a few spoonfuls of reserved cooking liquid.

Sprinkle with parsley and serve. It will not harm this dish for it to be reheated.

Laitues farcies à la bourbonnaise
BRAISED STUFFED LETTUCES

To serve 4 as a main course, or 8 as an accompaniment:
- 4 to 8 fat, leafy heads of Boston or butter lettuce (*see Note*)
- 5 ounces (1 quart, loosely packed) diced fresh bread, without crust
- ⅔ cup heavy cream
- 2 whole, poached chicken breasts, skin and bones removed
- 2 tablespoons chopped chives
- 2 tablespoons chopped parsley
- Salt
- Freshly ground pepper, preferably white
- 5 egg yolks
- 4 tablespoons butter, in all
- 1 small carrot, thinly sliced
- 1 onion, thinly sliced
- 3 tablespoons dry white wine
- 2 cups Chicken Stock (*fond blanc de volaille*, page 16)
- *Bouquet garni* (sprigs of thyme and parsley and a bay leaf, tied together)
- 1 pork skin (*this is usually readily available from any butcher specializing in pork products; Ed.*)

NOTE: *Depending on the size of the heads of lettuce, you may find yourself with a surplus of filling. Choose the number of lettuces accordingly and, if still uncertain, purchase a few extra heads. If you enjoy salad, they can hardly be wasted. If 4 large heads are sufficient and you wish to serve 8 portions, use a large sharp knife to cut carefully each cooked lettuce in half when they are ready to be served. Ed.*

HAVE READY:

1. The lettuces: Prepare the lettuces several hours before the final cooking time. Carefully trim the cores of the heads with the point of a sharp knife. Do not remove the cores completely and try to detach as few leaves as possible. Discard those that are blemished and save any others for salad. Wash the heads carefully.

Bring a large kettle of salted water to a rapid boil. Drop in the lettuces and cook them 3 to 4 minutes, depending on size. *(Because of size, you may have to cook only 2 or 3 heads at a time. Try to keep them submerged; they will tend to float. Depending on the quantity of water, the lettuces may be cooked, and ready for removal, before the water returns to a boil. Ed.)*

Lift out the lettuces with a skimmer. Place them directly into a colander, then plunge them into a large basin of ice water. Hold the lettuces by the core and swirl them in the water to remove all traces of sand. Press each head gently between your hands, then drain them well on a rack.

2. The filling (*la farce*): In a small mixing bowl, soak the bread in the cream.

Finely dice the chicken and mix it with the chives and parsley. Add salt and pepper to taste, then the cream-soaked bread.

Working quickly, with a wooden spoon, beat in the egg yolks all at once, then continue to beat the mixture until a uniform smoothness is obtained.

STUFFING THE LETTUCE:

Pat the lettuces gently with a paper towel and place them on a towel-covered work surface.

Without cutting through the core, divide each lettuce in two, from top to bottom. Spread them open and fill the interiors with the stuffing. Tuck some of the *farce* between the inner leaves as well as mounding it in the center.

Close the outer leaves over the filling, pressing them into place with your hands. Tie each head together with a string, first making a loop around the circumference, then adding a second loop from top to bottom.

COOKING:

Melt 2 tablespoons butter in the bottom of a heavy casserole large enough to contain all the packages of lettuce side by side. Add the carrots and onions and cook them, covered, for 5 minutes over low heat, stirring frequently.

Deglaze the casserole with white wine, place the lettuces on the vegetables, and pour the chicken stock over them. Push the *bouquet garni* deep into the center of the casserole, add salt and pepper, and cover completely with the pork skin. *(This will keep the lettuce a bright green. Cut the skin to fit the casserole, if necessary. Ed.)* Bring the liquid to a boil, then lower the heat to a simmer and cook, covered, 1 hour.

FINISHING THE LETTUCE:

Discard the pork skin and remove the lettuces. Drain them briefly, catching the juice and returning it to the casserole. Then place the lettuces on a lightly buttered platter. Cut and discard the string and cover the lettuces to keep them warm.

Remove the vegetables and *bouquet garni,* saving the carrots for decoration. Over high heat, boil down the cooking liquid until only about 6 tablespoons remain. Stir in 2 tablespoons butter, cut into tiny pieces, to thicken the sauce slightly.

Scatter the reserved carrots over the lettuces, and spoon the sauce over all. Serve at once. *(If necessary, the lettuces may be gently reheated in the butter sauce just before serving. Ed.)*

Gratin de pommes de terre à la forézienne
POTATOES COOKED IN CREAM

To serve 4:

 1¾ pounds waxy new potatoes
 Coarse salt
 Freshly ground pepper, preferably white
 1 cup milk
 1¼ cups *crème fraîche* (page 22)

PREPARATION:

Peel the potatoes at the last moment and slice them paper-thin. *(They should actually be transparent. Ed.)* Dry the potatoes well in a dish towel and mix them liberally with salt and pepper. *(Do this with your hands; because the slices cling together, it is the best method for distributing the seasonings evenly. Ed.)*

COOKING:

Bring the milk to a boil in a heavy casserole with high sides. Add the potatoes and return to the boiling point. Cover the casserole, reduce heat to low, and simmer 15 minutes.

After 15 minutes, the potatoes should have absorbed most of the milk. Add the *crème fraîche*, bring to a boil, re-cover the casserole, and turn heat to low. Cook the potatoes 45 minutes, stirring occasionally.

FINISHING THE POTATOES:

Preheat the broiler.

Transfer the potatoes to a shallow buttered casserole, or *au gratin* dish, and place them under the broiler for 10 minutes, or until nicely browned. Serve bubbling hot.

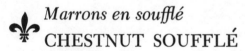

Marrons en soufflé
CHESTNUT SOUFFLÉ
(Color picture 12)

To serve 4:
    ¾ pound chestnuts
    Butter
    Flour
    1 cup milk
    1 teaspoon sugar
    ½ teaspoon salt
    3 tablespoons *crème fraîche* (page 22), or heavy cream
    5 egg whites
    3 egg yolks

HAVE READY:

1. The chestnuts: If possible, choose the large glossy variety called

bouches rouges, their shells tinged with red. Peel them according to the method given for Chestnut Purée (*purée mauve*, page 206).

2. The mold: Butter and lightly flour a soufflé dish about 7 inches in diameter with sides 3 inches high, or use 4 individual soufflé dishes 5 inches in diameter and 2½ inches high.

COOKING THE CHESTNUTS:

Put the peeled chestnuts in a small casserole with the milk, sugar, and salt. Boil gently, covered, for 10 minutes, then uncover, and cook 5 minutes longer, or until the milk has evaporated by at least half.

Reserve 4 whole chestnuts, and pass the rest through a fine sieve or food mill (*a food processor works very well for this operation; Ed.*) into a small casserole, and incorporate the *crème fraîche* (*see Note*). Keep the purée warm over very low heat while you beat the egg whites.

NOTE: *Cooked chestnuts can be very dry. If this is the case, do not hesitate to add more cream, even doubling the amount called for. Add enough so that the purée holds together in a thick paste. Ed.*

THE EGG WHITES:

In a copper bowl, beat the whites, either by hand with a wire whisk or with an electric beater. Add a pinch of salt and beat briskly until stiff but not dry.

PREPARATION OF THE SOUFFLÉ:

Heat the purée until gently bubbling, then stir in the egg yolks, one at a time. After a minute, remove the casserole from the heat.

Add one-quarter of the egg whites and blend them well with the purée.

Crumble 2 of the reserved chestnuts and add them to the mixture. Then, using a wooden or rubber spatula, fold the remaining whites into the purée, one half at a time. Fold them in lightly but swiftly until the blending is complete.

COOKING THE SOUFFLÉ:

Preheat oven to 375° F.

Scrape the soufflé mixture into the large prepared mold, or divide it among 4 individual soufflé dishes. Smooth the surface with a spatula and sprinkle with the remaining chestnuts, divided into 12 pieces.

Bake the soufflé 25 minutes or 15 minutes if you have prepared individual soufflés. Serve immediately.

Palets au potiron
FRIED PUMPKIN CAKES

To serve 4:
 1½ pounds fresh pumpkin
 Salt
 6 tablespoons flour
 2 eggs
 Zest of ¼ lemon, finely chopped
 Sugar
 Freshly ground pepper, preferably white
 2 tablespoons clarified butter (page 116, paragraph 2)
 Oil

PREPARATION OF THE PUMPKIN:

The evening before preparing this dish, cut the pumpkin into 4 pieces, scrape out the seeds, and peel it. Drop the pieces of pumpkin into a large casserole of boiling salted water, and cook from 15 to 30 minutes, depending on the degree of ripeness and the thickness of the flesh.

Drain the pumpkin, tie it up in several thicknesses of cheesecloth, and hang it over a deep bowl to drain overnight. (*Tie the cheesecloth to a dowel, or chopstick, slightly longer than the diameter of your bowl. Ed.*)

The next day, squeeze the cheesecloth to eliminate any excess water. There should be about 1½ cups of well-drained pulp. Pass the pulp through a fine sieve into a mixing bowl, pressing down on it with a wooden spoon.

Add the flour, eggs, lemon zest, salt, and a pinch of sugar. Then, give the mixture a few good turns of the pepper mill. Taste for seasoning and, using a wire whisk, incorporate the clarified butter, a little at a time. Chill the purée thoroughly in the refrigerator before cooking.

COOKING:

Five minutes before serving, heat a little oil in a frying pan. Using a teaspoon, form the cold pumpkin purée into small balls. Upon contact with the hot frying pan, they will spread like pancakes, and become approximately 2½ inches in diameter. Be sure to allow enough space between each ball so that they do not run together. Cook them for 30 seconds on each side.

TO SERVE:

Arrange the cakes in the shape of a crown, slightly overlapping, on a hot serving plate. They should be served as an accompaniment to meat with a highly seasoned sauce; or they may also be eaten sprinkled lightly with sugar as a dessert.

Pommes gaufrettes au beurre
CRISP RUFFLED POTATOES

To serve 4:

    1½ to 1¾ pounds Idaho potatoes
    1 teaspoon coarse salt
    ½ teaspoon freshly ground pepper
    12 tablespoons butter, clarified (page 116, paragraph 2)

PREPARE THE POTATOES:

Peel the potatoes and trim them into cylindrical shapes. Cut off and discard the rounded ends. Using the ruffled blade of a *mandoline,* or similar slicing device, cut the potatoes into thin, wavy slices, and drop them into a bowl of ice water. Soak the potatoes for 12 hours to crisp them. Change the water several times in order to wash away all traces of starch. (*If 12 hours' soaking time is not feasible, 8 hours will suffice. Ed.*)

COOKING:

Preheat oven to 500° F.

    Drain the potatoes and dry them thoroughly in a dish towel. Mix them well with salt and pepper, then coat them with warm clarified butter. Spread the potatoes out as evenly as possible in a large shallow roasting pan, or on a baking sheet, and place them in the hot oven for 20 minutes.

    Take the potatoes from the oven and, tilting the pan, pour off the butter. Hold a second, slightly smaller, baking pan over the potatoes to keep them in place.

FINISHING THE POTATOES:

Return the potatoes to the oven for 5 to 10 minutes, or until they become a crisp golden brown. Check them frequently to make sure they do not burn.

Serve the excess butter very hot as a sauce for grilled or pan-fried meats.

Pommes de terre "Mère Carles"
POTATOES ROASTED WITH BACON

To serve 4 to 6:

> 3 pounds small new potatoes, peeled (*see Note*)
> Salt
> Freshly ground pepper
> 14 thin slices of lean bacon (about ½ pound)
> 6 tablespoons butter, in all

NOTE: *28 tiny new potatoes would be ideal for this recipe, but may not be at hand when needed. In this case, divide 3 pounds of peeled new potatoes into 28 portions of equal size. In most instances, cutting them in half will do. Ed.*

PREPARE THE POTATOES AND BACON:

1. Place the potatoes in a large casserole, cover with cold water, add salt, and bring to a boil. Blanch them for 3 minutes, then drain in a colander. Dry the potatoes in a towel, and season with salt and pepper, mixing well.

2. Cut the 14 slices of bacon in half crosswise.

COOKING:

Preheat oven to 475° F.

Melt 3 tablespoons of butter in a heavy skillet large enough to hold the potatoes in one layer. Add the potatoes and cook them 20 minutes or longer, over medium to low heat. Shake the pan frequently and turn the potatoes often until they are evenly browned on all sides.

Remove the skillet from the stove and let the potatoes cool just enough so that they may be handled. Wrap the 28 browned potatoes with 28 pieces of bacon, joining, or nearly joining, each piece on the underside of the potato. Using the same skillet, place the wrapped potatoes in the oven for 10 minutes.

TO SERVE:

Drain off all cooking fat and replace it with the remaining 3 table-spoons of butter. *(The heat of the skillet will be sufficient to melt the butter. Ed.)* Roll the potatoes in this, putting any loose pieces of bacon back in place. Serve them on a hot plate, brushed with the freshly melted butter.

These potatoes make a nice accompaniment to roast veal or pan-fried meats.

Pommes de terre en robe de chambre soufflées
BAKED POTATO SOUFFLÉS

To serve 4:
    2 pounds Idaho potatoes of even size (*see Note*)
    4 tablespoons butter
    ½ cup *crème fraîche* (page 22)
    Salt
    Freshly ground pepper, preferably white
    2 eggs, separated
    4 ounces *jambon cru*, minced (*see Note*)
    1½ tablespoons chopped chives

NOTE: *For this recipe, use either 4 large potatoes, weighing 8 ounces each, or 8 smaller potatoes, weighing 4 ounces each.*

Raw ham, jambon cru *as it is referred to in France, is not to be confused with fresh pork. In this country Westphalian ham, sold by*

German butchers, comes close enough in flavor and texture to make a satisfactory substitute. If Westphalian ham is unobtainable, substitute Italian prosciutto. Ed.

COOKING THE POTATOES:

Preheat oven to 450° F.

Scrub the potatoes thoroughly and bake them 45 minutes to 1 hour, depending on size. (*Turn the potatoes halfway through the cooking time. Ed.*) Take the potatoes from the oven and reduce the temperature to 400° F.

PREPARATION OF THE SOUFFLÉS:

Thinking of the shape of a canoe, and using a small sharp knife, make an incision around the top (*actually one whole side*) of each potato, removing a lid encompassing three-quarters of the surface. Discard the lid, which will not be used. With a small spoon, carefully extract all the flesh until only a sturdy shell remains.

Purée the potato through a food mill using the fine blade, or push it through a sieve, into a small casserole. Place the casserole over low heat and add the butter, cut into small pieces; with a wooden spoon, work it into the potato.

Bring the *crème fraîche* to a boil, then incorporate it into the potato. Add salt and pepper to taste. The purée should be very fluffy.

Take the casserole from the heat and add the egg yolks, the minced ham, and then the chives, chopped at the last moment.

Beat the egg whites until just barely stiff and add them to the purée. Mix lightly and fill the potato shells. Arrange the soufflés on a baking sheet and place them in the 400° F. oven for 20 minutes.

Serve the potato soufflés immediately on a napkin-covered platter.

Purée de légumes stéphanoise
PURÉE OF FOUR VEGETABLES

NOTE: *The success of this dish depends on the freshness of the vegetables and on its being served as soon as possible after completion. In this case, reheating will destroy the delicate flavor achieved when the vegetables first come together with the butter after they have been puréed. Ed.*

To serve 4:
 ¼ pound tender young string beans, ends trimmed
 ½ pound fresh asparagus tips (*the first 2 inches of each stalk; Ed.*), cut into 1-inch pieces (out of season, canned white asparagus may be substituted)
 1½ pounds fresh young peas, to yield ½ pound shelled
 ¼ pound spinach (weight after all stems have been removed)
 5 tablespoons butter, in all
 Salt
 Freshly ground pepper
 ¼ teaspoon sugar (*optional*)

PREPARATION:

Cook the string beans and asparagus 7 minutes each, uncovered, in separate pans of boiling salted water. Drain, and quickly refresh them in a basin of ice water.

Put aside 15 string beans, cut into ¾-inch lengths, and 8 to 24 asparagus tips, depending on size.

Shell the peas at the last moment. Drop them into boiling salted water and cook 2 minutes, uncovered. Drain, and plunge them into ice water.

Put aside one-quarter of the peas with the reserved string beans and asparagus.

COOKING:

Melt 2 tablespoons of butter in a medium-size heavy casserole over low heat. Add the spinach and cook 5 minutes, covered.

Add the remaining quantities of string beans, asparagus, and peas. Cover the casserole tightly, and cook the vegetables for 30 minutes over low heat.

Then place the vegetables in a food mill, 1 cup at a time, and using the finest blade, purée them into a bowl. Discard any fibrous pieces that remain. Return the purée to the warm casserole in which the vegetables were cooked and cover it.

FINISHING THE PURÉE:

Heat a medium-size heavy skillet (*preferably enameled cast iron; Ed.*), and when it is very hot, swirl in the remaining 3 tablespoons of butter. Watch the butter carefully until it just begins to brown, then quickly stir in the purée, using a wooden spoon. Add salt and pepper to taste and a pinch of sugar.

If the purée must wait, put it in a double boiler and dot the surface with tiny pieces of butter to keep a crust from forming.

TO SERVE:

A moment before serving, reheat the reserved whole vegetables by dropping them into boiling salted water. Remove immediately and drain them well.

Present the purée in a warm, wide serving bowl. Sprinkle it with the hot vegetable *garniture* and serve at once. (*A wide serving bowl is important, in order not to have to pile on the vegetable garniture all in a clump. Ed.*)

Purée mauve
CHESTNUT PURÉE

To serve 6:
    2¼ pounds chestnuts
    3 cups milk
    7 tablespoons butter
    2 tablespoons cognac
    Coarse salt
    Sugar (*optional*)

PREPARATION OF THE CHESTNUTS:

Preheat oven to 500° F.

With the point of a small knife, make a gash, from top to bottom, across each chestnut. Be sure that there is a clean cut through the shell and the inner skin, without penetrating the nut itself too deeply.

Spread the chestnuts out on a large baking sheet and roast in the hot oven for 10 to 20 minutes. Turn them once or twice. When the shell separates from the chestnut, remove from the oven and, as soon as they are cool enough to handle, snap off the exterior shell, and peel off the interior skin.

NOTE: *The Troisgros' method for peeling chestnuts given on page 182, paragraph 3, is much easier than the roasting method they have given here. But, for this dish, there is a flavorful "toasty" quality gained by this procedure which to my mind is worth the extra labor. Ed.*

COOKING:

Place the chestnuts in a medium-size casserole and add milk. Cover, bring to a simmer, and cook about 30 minutes. *(Watch carefully that the milk does not boil over. Ed.)*

When the chestnuts are tender, pass them through a fine sieve, or food mill, with whatever cooking liquid remains. *(A food processor works very well for this. Ed.)*

Turn the purée into a clean casserole, and heat it, stirring constantly with a wooden spoon. *(If the purée is too thick, which is usually the case, add either more milk, cream, or rich stock, as you prefer. Ed.)*

A moment before serving, incorporate the cognac and the butter, cut into tiny pieces. Taste for seasoning, adding salt and, if desired, a pinch of sugar.

This purée is suggested as an accompaniment to game and roast pork.

Serpentins de légumes
VEGETABLE SERPENTINES

To serve 4:
>   2 large turnips, about 7 ounces each
>   2 large carrots, about 3 ounces each
>   1 large cucumber, about 7 ounces
>   7 tablespoons butter
>   Salt
>   Freshly ground pepper

For this recipe choose the largest vegetables available.

HAVE READY:

1. The turnips: Trim off the tops and bottoms of the turnips so that each becomes a cylinder 3 inches long, then peel them.

Using a sharp knife with a blade 3 inches long, turn the vegetable on its central axis to cut a thin ribbon of turnip as long as possible. If the band breaks, continue, as you should be able to use it all the same.

2. The carrots: After peeling the carrots, blanch them whole for 5 minutes to make them more flexible, then cut them into 3-inch lengths, and pare them into long bands the same way as the turnips.

3. The cucumbers: Peel and cut them the same way as the other vegetables, but stop at the first sign of seeds.

4. Plunge all these coils into boiling water for 1 minute, remove with a skimmer, and chill them briefly in ice water.

5. Superimpose the turnips, carrots, and cucumbers one upon another (in that order) to obtain tricolored bands 8 to 10 inches long. Roll them together into tight coils and tie them, like packages, with two strings. There should be 4 rolls each 3 inches long.

COOKING:

1. The vegetables: Drop the rolls into boiling salted water for 8 minutes.

2. The butter: In a small saucepan bring 3 tablespoons of water to a boil and stir in the butter, cut into tiny pieces, a little at a time. Beat with a wire whisk over high heat until a *liaison* is formed. Season the *beurre fondu* with salt and pepper.

TO SERVE:

Carefully lift the vegetables from the boiling water, remove the strings, and slice each roll crosswise into 3 equal pieces. Place around the edges of 4 hot plates and uncoil about a third of each piece to give the vegetables the appearance of streamers flying in the wind.

Dress the *serpentins* with *beurre fondu* and serve as quickly as possible.

We recommend that you use white plates which best enhance the color of the vegetables.

Tomates à la tomate
TOMATOES WITH TOMATO GARNITURE

To serve 4:
12 tomatoes, about 3 pounds in all
3 tablespoons butter, in all
2 onions, finely chopped
1 clove garlic, finely chopped
Bouquet garni (sprigs of thyme and parsley and a small bay leaf, tied together)
Coarse salt
Freshly ground pepper
3 tablespoons imported peanut oil
1 cup *crème fraîche* (page 22), or heavy cream

PREPARATION OF THE TOMATO SAUCE:

Drop 8 of the tomatoes into boiling water. Count to 10, then remove, and plunge them into cold water. When the tomatoes have chilled, peel them. Cut the tomatoes in half crosswise, and press lightly to remove the seeds. Then cut the flesh into uniform dice.

Melt 2 tablespoons of butter in a medium-size skillet over low heat, and sauté the onions until they are soft but not browned. Allow about 5 minutes for this. Add the diced tomato, garlic, *bouquet garni*, and a sprinkling of coarse salt. Bring the mixture to a boil, then reduce heat. Cover the skillet and cook 25 minutes, stirring occasionally.

Remove the *bouquet garni* and stir in the remaining tablespoon of butter. Add salt and pepper and taste for seasoning.

PREPARATION OF THE WHOLE TOMATOES:

Preheat oven to 375° F.

Cut the remaining 4 whole tomatoes in half crosswise. Heat the oil in a skillet until almost smoking and sauté the tomato halves, cut side down, for 3 minutes. Then turn, and place them in the oven for 10 minutes to finish cooking.

Take the tomatoes from the skillet and pour off all the oil, but do not clean the pan. Return the tomatoes to the skillet and add the *crème fraîche*. Simmer the tomatoes a few minutes over low heat, basting frequently with the cream.

TO SERVE:

Arrange the 8 tomato halves on a warm serving platter. Nap with the *crème fraîche* and surround them with the hot diced-tomato *garniture*.

Coquillettes aux truffes "Jolly Martine"
PASTA SHELLS WITH TRUFFLES

To serve 4:
    8 ounces tiny pasta shells
    1½ ounces truffles
    Salt
    3 to 8 tablespoons truffle juice
    7 tablespoons butter

HAVE READY:

1. The pasta shells: If the pasta shells are not freshly made, then buy the best imported shells available. They should be of the smallest size (*conchigliettes*) and made with eggs.

2. The truffles: If you can find fresh truffles (from January through February), cook them for 20 minutes, covered, in a little salted water.

If you use canned truffles, try to buy those that are processed only once for canning, called *de première cuisson* on the label. In either case, peel the truffles and cut them into uniform *julienne* strips. Reserve from 3 to 8 tablespoons of the truffle cooking liquid or juice from the can; you may have anywhere from 3 to 8 tablespoons.

COOKING:

Bring 3 quarts of salted water to a rapid boil. Then drop in the pasta, stirring simultaneously with a fork to make certain the shells do not stick together. (*The addition of a tablespoon of butter or oil will help prevent this problem. Ed.*)

Cook the pasta, uncovered, for 10 to 14 minutes, or until it is just done (*al dente*). Check frequently and, the moment it is ready, add a cup of cold water to stop the cooking. Drain the pasta immediately, in a colander.

Pour the truffle juice into a medium-size, heatproof serving dish or casserole, and boil down until the bottom of the casserole is nearly dry. Then, add the drained pasta and the butter, cut into tiny pieces. Stir the pasta with a cooking fork over low heat, until the butter thickens and forms a *liaison.*

Carefully incorporate the *julienne* strips of truffle without breaking them, and serve immediately.

Nouilles au lard

FRESH NOODLES WITH BACON AND TOMATO

To serve 4:
    12 ounces fresh noodles (*see Note*)
    ½ pound fresh (unsmoked) bacon, in one piece
    2 pounds tomatoes
    2 cloves garlic, finely chopped
    8 fresh mint leaves (*fresh basil leaves may be substituted; Ed.*)
    Coarse salt
    Freshly ground pepper

HAVE READY:

1. Cut 1 ounce of fresh noodles into 1-inch pieces. Set them aside.

If you would prefer to dispense with making your own fresh noodles, they can often be bought in specialty shops.

NOTE: *In the United States, fresh noodles are usually sold in Italian neighborhoods, but they can also frequently be found in Oriental markets. If necessary, this recipe can be prepared with the best quality of imported dry noodles. However, you will then have to eliminate the fried noodle garniture. Ed.*

2. Remove the rind from the fresh bacon and cut the bacon into *lardons* about 1 inch long and ¼ inch thick. Place them in a saucepan, cover with cold water, and bring to a boil. Blanch the *lardons* for 3 minutes, then drain them in a sieve.

3. Drop the tomatoes into boiling water. Count to 10, drain, and plunge them into cold water. Peel and seed the tomatoes, squeezing out excess water, then pass them through a fine sieve or a food mill.

COOKING:

Turn the sieved tomatoes into a medium-size saucepan, add the garlic and mint leaves, and bring to a boil. Cook the sauce for 5 minutes, then cool slightly, and remove the mint leaves.

Lightly brown the *lardons* in a small skillet over low heat. Allow 20 to 30 minutes for this operation. Remove the *lardons* with half of their cooking fat and set them aside.

Fry 1 ounce of the cut fresh noodles in the remaining fat for about 3 minutes, or until crisp and nicely browned. Plan to cook the remaining pasta at the last moment and to serve the dish at once.

Plunge the remaining 11 ounces of noodles into a large kettle of boiling salted water. Cook 7 to 8 minutes, or until just done (*al dente*). Stop the cooking with a cup of cold water and drain the noodles immediately in a colander. (*The cooking time varies extensively with fresh noodles, depending upon their thickness. Begin to check on their degree of doneness after 3 minutes. Ed.*)

While the noodles are cooking, return the tomato sauce to the stove to warm over very low heat. Do the same with the *lardons*.

FINISHING THE NOODLES:

As soon as the pasta has been well drained, return it to the hot kettle in which it was cooked. Pour the tomato sauce over it and add the bacon with its extra fat. Add a liberal grinding of pepper, taste for salt, and mix well with a large fork.

Turn the noodles into a wide heated serving bowl and sprinkle them with the crisp fried noodles. Serve at once.

Les desserts

DESSERTS

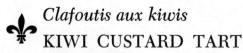

Clafoutis aux kiwis

KIWI CUSTARD TART

(Color picture 8)

To serve 8:

    ½ pound Sweet Pastry Dough (½ recipe *pâte sucrée*, page 32)

    2 eggs

    1 cup *crème fraîche* (page 22), or heavy cream

    6 tablespoons superfine sugar, in all

    3 tablespoons *eau de vie de prune* (*not sold in the United States;*
        substitute eau de vie de mirabelle, *or kirsch; Ed.*)

    7 to 10 kiwis, depending on size

HAVE READY:

1. The pastry: Roll the pastry out into a circle large enough to line a false-bottomed tart mold, or pastry ring, with a diameter of 11 inches. Chill until ready to bake.

2. The custard: In a mixing bowl, combine the eggs, *crème fraîche*, 5 tablespoons of sugar, and *eau de vie*. Using a wire whisk, or rotary eggbeater, mix until well blended. Refine the custard by passing it through a fine sieve.

3. The kiwis: Peel the kiwis and cut them into slices ½ inch thick.

COOKING:

Preheat oven to 425° F.

Line the tart shell with wax paper and weigh down the dough with dried beans or rice. Prebake the pastry 12 minutes, then remove the beans and wax paper, and bake for 5 minutes longer to dry the bottom of the shell.

Lower oven temperature to 350° F.

Decorate the bottom of the pastry with sliced kiwis, then pour the custard mixture over them. Bake the tart for 20 minutes, then reduce the heat to 325° F. and bake it 5 minutes longer.

Preheat the broiler.

Remove the tart from the oven and sprinkle it with the remaining tablespoon of sugar. Place it under the broiler for just long enough to caramelize the sugar. If necessary, protect the edges of the tart with a strip of aluminum foil.

Slip the *clafoutis* out of its mold onto a serving plate. Serve either hot or cold.

Gouïre aux myrtilles dans la feuille de chou
BILBERRY COBBLER IN A CABBAGE LEAF

NOTE: *I have been told that* myrtilles *(bilberries) are abundant in the wild, particularly in Maine. Since it is unlikely that one would find bilberries marketed, huckleberries may be substituted, and so may blueberries, which are of the same family.*

The thought of preparing a dessert in a cabbage leaf may strike you as peculiar, but the effect is most attractive. The brilliant purple of the cooked berries against the protruding green of the cabbage leaf resembles a cluster of grapes on the vine. Ed.

To serve 4:
    3 perfect cabbage leaves
    8 to 10 ounces bilberries, huckleberries, or blueberries
    2 eggs
    2 tablespoons flour
    4 tablespoons sugar
    3 tablespoons *crème fraîche* (page 22)
    2 tablespoons butter

HAVE READY:

1. The cabbage: Take 3 beautiful leaves from the exterior of the cabbage, choosing the largest, and blanch them for 10 minutes in a kettle of boiling salted water. Drain, and dry them with a towel.

2. The bilberries: Pick over the berries, taking care to remove any leaves or small stems.

3. The batter: Mix the eggs, flour, sugar, and *crème fraîche* in a bowl. Refine the batter by straining it through a fine sieve.

COOKING:

Preheat oven to 425° F.

Melt the butter over low heat in a heavy cast-iron skillet about 9 inches in diameter with curved sides. Roll the cabbage leaves in the butter before spreading them out over the bottom and sides of the skillet.

Fill the leaves with berries and pour the batter on top. Place the skillet in the oven and lower the heat to 400° F. Bake the cobbler 15 minutes, then remove it from the oven and, if necessary, finish cooking the cabbage on top of the stove. The cabbage covering the bottom of the skillet should take on a beautiful golden crispness. You can check its progress by lifting it slightly with a spatula.

Gently slide the cobbler onto a serving plate and wait 15 minutes for it to settle, then serve while still hot. (*The cobbler with its edging of green against a black iron skillet may also be presented as is. Ed.*)

Coffret de cerises Lamartine
BRIOCHE STUFFED WITH CHERRIES

To serve 4:

    60 cherries (1 pound), ripe but firm
    ¾ cup red currant jelly
    3 tablespoons kirsch
    1-pound brioche baked in a rectangular bread mold (either make
        it yourself or buy it from a bakery)
    Powdered sugar

PREPARING THE CHERRY COMPOTE:

Pit the cherries, using a cherry pitter.

Place the jelly in a heavy saucepan with high sides and thin it with ⅜ cup water. Bring this to a boil and drop in the cherries. Cover and cook 3 minutes. (*Warning! The heat will have to be lowered and adjusted so that the syrup does not boil over. Give this your constant attention. Ed.*)

With a slotted spoon or skimmer, remove the cherries from the syrup and set them aside in a serving compote.

Return the saucepan to high heat and boil down the syrup until it is reduced to about ¾ cup.

Off the heat, add the kirsch, which must not be·allowed to boil in order to preserve its perfume.

PREPARING THE *coffrets* OF BRIOCHE:

Starting at the center of the loaf, cut the brioche into slices 1 inch thick. Trim the slices into rectangles 3 inches by 5 inches. (*If your brioche already conforms to these dimensions, just trim off the crust, which would char under the grill. Ed.*)

With the point of a knife, make an incision around each piece of brioche about ½ inch in from the edge and ½ inch deep. This is to facilitate the removal of a lid after the slices are glazed.

Preheat the broiler.

Arrange the *coffrets* on a baking sheet, scored side up. Dust with sieved powdered sugar and caramelize them under the broiler. Turn them and do the same to the bottom sides. Then, with the point of a small knife, carefully lift off the covers of the boxes, following their outlines.

TO SERVE:

Spoon the reduced syrup into the centers of 4 plates. Place the *coffrets* on top. Fill the interior of each with cherries and cover with its lid. This dessert should be eaten while it is still warm.

Le grand dessert Troisgros

POACHED AND FRESH FRUITS WITH ICES AND RASPBERRY SAUCE

(Color picture 8)

This dessert is an assortment of fruits which will vary depending on the season. It is essential to have the choicest fresh fruits and as many different varieties as possible. They are to be served with sherbet and ice cream, all brought together with a light brushing of raspberry sauce and, if desired, *crème fraîche* (page 22).

PREPARATION OF THE POACHED FRUIT:

1. The syrup: Make a syrup with the proportions of 1½ cups sugar to 1 quart water. Simmer until the sugar is dissolved.

The quantity of syrup must be sufficient to cover the fruits entirely, and the cooking times will vary depending on the degree of ripeness of each fruit.

2. Peaches: Peel the peaches; if necessary, blanch for 10 seconds in boiling water to facilitate the removal of their skin. Poach the peaches whole in the syrup, then cut them in half and remove the pit.

3. Pears: Peel the pears and wipe the flesh with a cut lemon to prevent darkening. Halve them, and remove the stems, cores, and seeds. Poach the pears in syrup, then cut the pieces in half again.

4. Cherries: Pit the cherries and tie them together in a sack of cheesecloth. Cook them briefly in rapidly boiling syrup.

5. Apricots: Cut them in half and remove the pit. Poach the apricots with a stick of cinnamon added to the syrup.

6. Plums: Cook the plums whole in syrup.

7. Prunes: Soak the prunes in water overnight, then place them in a pan of cold water and bring to a boil. At the first sign of a simmer, remove the prunes, and drain them in a sieve. Then cut them in half and extract the pit.

8. Figs: Poach the figs in red wine with a little sugar and 2 bay leaves.

PREPARATION OF THE UNCOOKED FRUIT:

1. Fresh almonds: Shell the almonds and split them in half.

2. Grapes: Remove the seeds.

3. Melon: Cut the melon in half and remove the seeds. Then carve the melon into small balls, using either a spoon or a melon-ball cutter. Take care not to get too close to the rind. Marinate the balls in a little sugar (*optional*) and orange liqueur.

4. Pineapple: Peel the pineapple, cut it into thick slices, then cut the slices into small wedges. Marinate the pineapple in cold syrup.

5. Oranges and grapefruit: Peel the fruit close to the flesh, removing all the white pith. Using a small sharp knife, cut between the pulp and membranes to separate each segment. Do this over a bowl to catch the juice. Marinate the segments in their own juice for 24 hours. If you wish, add a little sugar.

6. Red fruits:

Strawberries: Remove the stems from the berries, wash them if necessary, then sprinkle with a little sugar and lemon juice. If they are large, cut them in half.

Wild strawberries, raspberries, blackberries: Do not damage these by washing unless absolutely necessary.

THE RASPBERRY SAUCE (*coulis de framboise*):

To serve 4:

    8 ounces fresh raspberries (*see Note*)
    ½ cup sugar, or to taste

Pass the fresh raspberries through a food mill into a glass receptacle. Sprinkle the purée with sugar, then chill it in the refrigerator. Stir the sauce occasionally with a wooden spoon to dissolve the sugar.

NOTE: *Frozen raspberries may be used in place of fresh with satisfactory results. In this case, thaw two 10-ounce packages in a sieve, and discard the sugar syrup, or save it for another use. Do not add sugar. Ed.*

ASSEMBLING THE *grand dessert*:

Have a large, well-chilled serving platter ready. Place a heaping spoonful of sherbet (Cactus-fruit, page 231; or strawberry, raspberry, or pineapple) in the center of the platter, then place another spoonful of ice cream next to it (Walnut, page 220; or vanilla or honey).

Surround the ices with the fresh and poached fruits of the season, arranged harmoniously by color and brushed lightly with raspberry sauce, or with small dollops of *crème fraîche* (use either very little cream or none at all).

On a separate platter, present small portions of other desserts such as Kiwi Custard Tart (page 214) and Three-layer Chocolate Cake (page 236).

Decorate your dining table with small plates of Caramelized Puff-pastry Spirals (page 222), Oversized Almond Wafers (page 239), Candied Grapefruit Peel (page 227), and glazed chestnuts. You might also include macaroons of assorted flavors.

Glace aux noix
WALNUT ICE CREAM

To serve 4:
    ½ cup freshly shelled walnut meats
    5 egg yolks
    ¾ cup black-locust honey (*miel d'acacia*)
    2 cups heavy cream
    Salt
    1 vanilla bean or 1 tablespoon vanilla extract

HAVE READY:

1. The walnuts: Choose fresh healthy walnuts. Shell them at the last moment, remove the nut meats, and peel off all the paperlike skins with a small sharp knife. Then chop the meats coarsely.

2. The egg yolks: Mix the yolks in a bowl with the honey, then beat them for at least 5 minutes with a wire whisk, or until they are thick enough to form a ribbon. (*I suggest using an electric mixer or beater. Ed.*)

PREPARATION OF THE ICE CREAM:

In a heavy saucepan, bring the cream to a simmer. Add the chopped walnuts with a dash of salt (*and a vanilla bean, if you are using one; Ed.*), and reduce the heat to as low as possible. Let the walnuts steep in the cream for 10 minutes to produce an infusion.

Beating constantly, pour the hot cream over the yolk mixture, and continue to beat until the custard is thick enough to coat a spoon. If necessary, beat the eggs and cream over hot water (*bain-marie*) held below a simmer. Then pour the mixture into a cold mixing bowl and continue beating until it is cool. (Add vanilla extract if you did not use a vanilla bean.) Chill well in the refrigerator.

FINISHING THE ICE CREAM:

No more than 30 minutes before you plan to serve the ice cream, crank it in an ice-cream freezer according to the manufacturer's directions.

Millet au potiron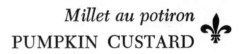
PUMPKIN CUSTARD

To serve 6:
    1½ pounds fresh pumpkin
    Salt
    1½ tablespoons butter
    5 tablespoons flour
    3½ tablespoons sugar
    3 eggs
    1 cup milk
    3 tablespoons *crème fraîche* (page 22), or heavy cream
    3 tablespoons dark raisins, soaked in cold water
    Freshly grated nutmeg
    Finely ground white pepper
    Zest of ½ lemon, either grated or minced

PREPARATION OF THE PUMPKIN:

Choose a ripe pumpkin, preferably orange. (*In France pumpkins are often a vermilion red. Ed.*) Cut it into large pieces, remove the seeds, and peel the pieces. Drop the pumpkin into a large casserole of lightly salted boiling water and cook for 10 minutes, then drain in a colander.

Melt the butter in a large sauté pan and add the pumpkin. Stirring frequently, cook until all the water has evaporated and the pumpkin becomes a purée. (*This will take about 30 minutes. Ed.*)

In a large mixing bowl, combine the flour, sugar, eggs, milk, and *crème fraîche*. Mix briefly with a wire whisk, then incorporate the pumpkin purée. Drain the raisins, and add them to the mixture with a sprinkling of freshly grated nutmeg, a pinch of white pepper, and the lemon zest.

COOKING:

Preheat oven to 350° F.

Spoon the pumpkin mixture into a 6-inch-by-9-inch shallow baking dish with sides about 2½ inches high. Place the baking dish in a larger pan of hot water and bake 45 minutes.

TO SERVE:

Cool the pudding and chill it in the refrigerator for 2 to 3 hours. When ready to serve, mound it in individual dessert dishes as you would an ice cream or mousse. *(This dessert has the consistency of a mousse. Ed.)*

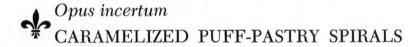

Opus incertum

CARAMELIZED PUFF-PASTRY SPIRALS

To serve 8:
   ½ pound Puff Pastry (*pâte feuilletée*, page 32)
   6 tablespoons sugar, in all
   2 tablespoons powdered sugar

PREPARATION OF THE DOUGH:

Make the puff pastry the day before and set aside one-quarter of it, in the refrigerator, for this confection. *(Freeze the remainder. Ed.)*

The next day, spread 2 tablespoons of sugar over your work surface, and give the dough a seventh turn, incorporating the sugar as if it were flour. Then, sprinkle the pastry with 2 more tablespoons of sugar, and give it an eighth, and final, turn. The sugar should be completely incorporated into the dough. Refrigerate the dough for 30 minutes.

BUILDING THE SPIRALS:

After 30 minutes, roll the pastry out into a rectangle approximately 8 inches long, simultaneously sprinkling it with the remaining 2 table-spoons of sugar.

Cut the dough crosswise into 3 equal pieces each about 2½ inches wide. Using a pastry brush, moisten the bands of dough with a little water, then stack them one on top of the other. Tap the stack lightly with the rolling pin to make sure the 3 layers adhere, then place the block of dough in the freezer for 15 to 20 minutes. This will make it easier to slice the pastry one more time.

NOTE: *Now the dough is to be cut one more time, and then the arrangement of the pieces will account for the name,* opus incertum, *of the pastry. The reference is to a type of ancient Roman facing for masonry; there are many such definitions in Roman architecture. The* incertum *variety is an irregular facing of stone or brick. Think of the 5 pieces of pastry you are about to arrange together as 5 bricks set in a vertical pattern on the baking sheet; it is irregular in the sense that there are spaces between some of the "bricks." Ed.*

FINISHING THE PASTRY:

Preheat oven to 450° F.

Cover a lightly oiled baking sheet with a piece of parchment paper, then dust it with powdered sugar, sifting the sugar through a fine sieve. With your fingers sprinkle a little water over all.

Remove the dough from the freezer and cut it crosswise into 5 equal strips; these "bricks" should now be about ½ inch thick. Turn them so that one side on which you can see the layering of the dough is uppermost, and arrange 2 pieces on the baking sheet, parallel to each other on their long sides and about 1 inch apart. Set the third brick directly under the 1-inch space and just touching the first 2 bricks; this piece, and the 2 to follow, must head in the same up-and-down direction as the first ones. Now align the last 2 pieces below and touching the bottom of the third piece, with the same 1-inch space between them that the first pair has. The effect is of a tall, narrow letter *H*.

Bake the pastry for 15 minutes. The 5 oblong pieces will have expanded and rounded out somewhat and should have merged together around the center piece. Turn all 5 over together, maneuvering them with 2 large spatulas. Then lower the oven temperature to 400° F., and bake the pastry for 5 minutes longer. Turn off the oven and let the pastry remain inside 5 more minutes; check to make sure that it does not scorch during this time.

When the baking is completed, the pastry should have expanded into 5 connected pieces each with a visible, caramelized spiral pattern similar to a classic *palmier*. Let it cool on the baking sheet for 30 minutes.

TO SERVE:

Cover a silver platter with a white napkin, and place the pastry on the napkin, taking care to keep it in one piece. The platter is set in the center of the table for guests to help themselves. breaking off pieces of the spirals with their fingers. *(The recipe will serve 8, but the pastry is easily consumed by only 4. Ed.)*

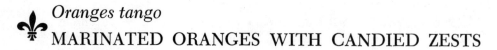

Oranges tango

MARINATED ORANGES WITH CANDIED ZESTS

To serve 6:
   8 navel oranges
   3 tablespoons Grand Marnier
   2 teaspoons sugar (*optional*)
   7 tablespoons grenadine syrup

HAVE READY:

1. The zests: Choose large seedless navel oranges that have not been sprayed or treated. Navels are in season from November to April. Cut the zest into thin *julienne* strips and drop them into a

large amount of boiling water. Boil vigorously for 15 minutes. Drain the zests in a sieve, then plunge them into cold water, and drain again.

2. The oranges: Using a small sharp knife, peel the oranges close to the flesh, removing all traces of white pith. Hold the oranges over a bowl, and section them, slicing between the pulp and the membranes. Drop the segments into the bowl and squeeze out any juices left in the membrane before discarding it.

Add the Grand Marnier and 2 teaspoons of sugar. *(Use less sugar if the oranges are very sweet. Ed.)* Toss the oranges briefly and marinate them in the refrigerator for at least 3 hours. While they are chilling, toss them again several times.

COOKING THE ZESTS:

In a small heavy saucepan, bring the grenadine syrup to a boil. Drop in the zests, stir until they are completely coated, then reduce the heat to barely a simmer. Cook the zests about 1 hour, stirring frequently, or until all liquid has evaporated and the zests have become a sticky confection. Set them aside.

TO SERVE:

Serve the ice-cold orange segments in individual chilled glass bowls, or from a large glass compote, sprinkled with the candied zests.

Oreillettes
DEEP-FRIED PASTRIES WITH LEMON
AND RUM

To make about 20 pastries:
    1¾ cups flour
    2 teaspoons baking powder
    ¼ teaspoon salt
    6 tablespoons sugar
    3 tablespoons butter
    2 egg yolks

2 tablespoons rum
Zest of ½ lemon, grated
1 quart oil for deep frying
Powdered sugar

PREPARATION OF THE DOUGH:

Sift together the flour, baking powder, salt, and sugar into a mixing bowl. Cut the butter into tiny pieces, then blend it into the flour using a pastry blender or two forks.

Make a deep well in the flour mixture, and put in it the egg yolks, rum, and lemon zests. Without combining with the flour, stir the yolks with either your fingers or the point of a knife. Then add 3 tablespoons of ice water, and begin to work the flour with your fingers into the wet ingredients.

As soon as the dough begins to come together, scrape it out of the bowl onto a lightly floured work surface (preferably cold marble), and knead briefly. Do not overwork the dough. Stop as soon as it has body and elasticity.

Form the dough into a ball, cover it with a damp napkin, and let rest 1 hour in the refrigerator.

FORMING THE *oreillettes*:

Using a rolling pin, give the dough 2 turns (see page 34), rolling out and folding the dough twice. Then roll it to a final thickness of about ¼ inch and cut it into diamond shapes about 4 inches by 2½ inches. With the back of a knife, gently indent a design to your own taste on the surface of the diamonds.

COOKING:

In a casserole, heat the oil for deep frying to 360° F.

Drop the *oreillettes* into the oil, a few at a time, and fry for about 1 minute. As soon as the bottom side has browned, turn them to the second side. Drain the *oreillettes* on paper towels, then roll them in powdered sugar.

These pastries may be eaten warm or cold and may be kept for 2 to 3 days in an air-tight container.

Pamélas ⚜

CANDIED GRAPEFRUIT PEEL

(Color picture 8)

To make 6 to 8 dozen candied grapefruit peels:
    4 to 6 grapefruit, about 4 pounds
    2¾ cups (1¼ pounds) superfine sugar
    ¼ pound crystallized rock sugar, crushed (*see Note*)

PREPARATION OF THE GRAPEFRUIT:

Choose thick-skinned grapefruit. Cut off the two extremities, then divide the grapefruit into quarters from top to bottom. Using a sharp knife, make a clean sweep, removing the peel but leaving a third of the pulp attached to the rind.

Cut each of the quarters of peel lengthwise into 4 equal strips. Each fruit should yield 16 strips about 3 inches long and ¾ inch thick.

COOKING:

Place the prepared peel in a large casserole, add cold water to cover well, and slowly bring to a boil, uncovered. Boil rapidly for 5 minutes, then drain the peel in a colander. Repeat this procedure 4 times, beginning with cold water each time. This blanching removes all but a pleasing trace of bitterness from the peel.

Return the peel to the same casserole; this time do not add water. Mix in the superfine sugar, and cook, uncovered, over very low heat, turning the peel frequently with a wooden spoon. It is important that this operation be done very slowly. If the liquid evaporates too fast, the peel will be insufficiently cooked. Allow between 1 and 2 hours to glaze it.

TO FINISH:

Arrange the candied grapefruit on racks set over wax paper, so that excess syrup may drain away.

When cool enough to handle, take the peel, one piece at a time, and roll it in crushed crystallized sugar.

Enjoy the candied peel as soon as it is cool.

NOTE: *In the United States, one does not usually find crystallized* *rock sugar available crushed. The solution is to buy clear, crystallized rock-sugar candy and to crush it with a mortar and pestle, a hammer, or in a food processor or a blender. Be sure to remove the thread that usually holds rock candy together.*

FOR BREAKFAST THE NEXT DAY:

To enjoy the remaining fresh grapefruit, use a small sharp knife to cut the flesh into sections, and remove all membrane and seeds. Place the segments in a bowl and squeeze over them any juices remaining in the membrane.

Sprinkle the grapefruit lightly with sugar and let chill in the refrigerator overnight.

Serve this for *petit déjeuner* in chilled individual bowls, accompanied by very lightly sugared coffee.

Pêches et amandes au Brouilly

PEACHES AND ALMONDS IN RED WINE

(Color picture 8)

To serve 4:

    10 peaches, about 2 pounds
    24 shelled fresh almonds, about ⅓ cup
    8 ounces raspberries (*see Note*)
    1 cup Beaujolais, preferably a Brouilly (or other light, dry red wine)
    ¼ cup sugar

PREPARATION:

1. The almonds: Shell the almonds, then blanch them in boiling water for 1 minute. Drain them and remove the skins by pinching the almonds between your fingers.

Stick the point of a small knife through the center of each almond lengthwise, splitting them in half.

2. The raspberries: Press the berries through a fine sieve or food mill, collecting the purée in a small bowl. Discard the seeds.

NOTE: *If necessary, frozen raspberries may be used. In this case, use two 10-ounce packages. Thaw them in a sieve and discard their syrup, or save it for another use. Do not add sugar. Ed.*

3. The peaches: Peel the peaches with a small knife. If they are ripe enough, the skin should pull away easily. Cut the peaches into eighths, remove the pit, and place them in a bowl.

4. Mix the red wine with the raspberry purée. Stir in the sugar and pour it over the peaches. Chill the fruit in the refrigerator for 1 hour.

TO SERVE:

Divide the peaches and wine among 4 large, ice-cold stemmed wine goblets and sprinkle them with the almonds. Provide dessert spoons of appropriate size.

If you do not have large glasses of the right size and shape, the peaches may be arranged in glass ramekins imbedded in crushed ice.

Pruneaux au rasteau et la crème fraîche
PRUNES POACHED IN WINE

To serve 6 or 8:
  2 pounds prunes, about 36 pieces
  2 cups *vin de rasteau*, a sweet red dessert wine from the Rhône
    Valley (*see Note*)
  2 cups light red Bordeaux
  1 orange
  1 lemon
  ¾ cup raspberry juice (*see Note*)
  3 tablespoons sugar (*optional*)
  ¾ cup *crème fraîche* (page 22)

NOTE: Vin de rasteau *is unavailable in the United States, as is true of many sweet dessert wines* (vins doux) *of France. Yet, there are two* *alternatives, wines that are available here and with which this recipe can succeed. One alternative is to combine 2 cups of white port with 2 cups of a light red Bordeaux or Beaujolais. The other is to substitute 4 cups of sweet (recioto) Italian Valpolicella for both the* rasteau *and* Bordeaux.

If fresh raspberries are not in season, thaw one or two 10-ounce packages of frozen raspberries and press out their juice. In this case, do not add the sugar. Ed.

PREPARATION:

Place the prunes in a glass bowl, add the wine, and let them soak overnight.

The next day, when the prunes have swelled, place them in a glass or enameled casserole with the wine, and add thin, unpeeled slices of orange and lemon. Stir in the raspberry juice and then sugar, if needed. (*Taste before adding sugar. Ed.*) Bring the liquid just to a simmer, reduce the heat to low, and cook the prunes for 15 minutes. Stir occasionally.

Cool the prunes and refrigerate them for 3 days in their cooking liquid.

TO SERVE:

Remove the slices of orange and lemon and serve the chilled prunes in small deep plates with some of the wine. At the last moment, top them with a large dollop of *crème fraîche.*

NOTE: *I found that these prunes could also be served as a delicious accompaniment to roast pork. They can be kept for at least 6 weeks under refrigeration and so are convenient to have on hand.*

Sorbet à la figue de Barbarie
CACTUS-FRUIT SHERBET

To serve 6:

    2¾ pounds cactus fruit ("prickly pears")
    ¾ cup sugar, in all
    1½ tablespoons kirsch
    Juice of 1 lemon
    ⅓ cup heavy cream

PREPARATION:

Choose the fruit just ripe and unblemished. Handling this fruit can be delicate work if its covering of fine nettlelike needles has not been previously removed. If this is the case, wear gloves while peeling them. With a small sharp knife, cut off each end of the fruit, then pull away the skin. It should separate easily from the flesh. Cut 3 of the pears into thick slices, put these in a bowl with 1½ tablespoons of sugar and the kirsch, and marinate them in the refrigerator.

Pass the rest of the fruit through the fine blade of a food mill, catching the pulp and liquid in a mixing bowl. Add the lemon juice and ½ cup of sugar. Stir until combined, then place the mixture in the refrigerator to chill.

Beat the cream in a bowl over ice until it becomes very thick. Slowly add the remaining sugar and then the chilled puréed fruit.

Finish the *sorbet* in an ice-cream maker, following the manufacturer's directions.

NOTE: *If an ice-cream maker is not available, you can improvise by pouring the mixture into a shallow metal pan. Place in the freezer and stir frequently with the tines of a fork until set. Then, stir again occasionally to give sherbet texture and volume. Ed.*

TO SERVE:

Mound the *sorbet* in a cold glass bowl and decorate it with the marinated slices of cactus fruit.

⚜ *Crème patissière pour soufflé*
PASTRY CREAM FOR SOUFFLES

To make about 1½ cups:
    2 eggs
    7 tablespoons sugar
    4 tablespoons flour
    1 cup milk
    3 egg yolks

PREPARATION:

Beat the eggs lightly in a mixing bowl and, using a wire whisk, incorporate the sugar and the flour.

In a heavy saucepan, bring the milk to a boil. Pour it over the egg mixture and, stirring continuously, pour the mixture back into the saucepan. Continue to cook, stirring, for 2 to 3 minutes, then rub the thickened pastry cream through a fine sieve into the top of a double boiler (*bain-marie*). Beat in the egg yolks until thoroughly incorporated, and keep the mixture warm until ready to use.

⚜ *Soufflé flambé aux pralines*
PRALINE SOUFFLE

To serve 4:
    1¼ cups coarsely crushed pralines (*see Note*)
    Butter
    Sugar
    8 egg whites
    Salt
    ⅔ cup warm Pastry Cream for Soufflés (*crème pâtissière pour soufflé*, above)
    3 tablespoons orange liqueur, preferably Grand Marnier
    1 pint praline ice cream

HAVE READY:

1. The praline: Lay the pralines on your work surface and crush them coarsely with a rolling pin.

NOTE: *In case pralines are not easily available, they are very simple to prepare: Roast 1 cup blanched almonds in a 350° F. oven until lightly browned. Dissolve ½ cup sugar in 3 tablespoons water in a heavy sauce-pan and cook, swirling the pan, until caramelized.*

Stir in the almonds, then quickly spread the praline out on an oiled baking sheet to harden. After 30 minutes, crack the praline into manageable pieces. Ed.

2. Rub a 14-inch oval *au gratin* dish liberally with butter, then coat with sugar, tilting the dish back and forth until evenly coated. Turn the dish over to remove any excess sugar.

PREPARATION OF THE SOUFFLÉ:

Preheat oven to 400° F.

Add a pinch of salt to the egg whites and beat them with a wire whisk (*or use an electric mixer; Ed.*) in a copper bowl until stiff but not dry.

As soon as the whites hold, mix one-quarter of them into the warm pastry cream, stirring until completely blended. Then return the mixture to the remaining whites and fold them together with a wooden spoon or spatula until evenly combined.

Incorporate the crushed praline into the batter, but reserve ¼ cup of it.

Spread the soufflé batter over the prepared *au gratin* dish and scatter the reserved praline on top.

Place the soufflé in the oven and, after closing the oven door, reduce the heat to 375° F. Bake the soufflé for 16 minutes, bring it quickly to the table, and sprinkle with the orange liqueur.

Ignite the liqueur and, as it burns, poke holes with a pointed knife in the surface of the soufflé, and tilt the dish back and forth so that the liqueur can penetrate the interior.

Serve immediately, accompanied by praline ice cream.

Tarte au melon
CANTALOUPE TART

To serve 4:

½ pound Sweet Pastry Dough (½ recipe *pâte sucrée*, page 32)
3 cantaloupes, about 1⅓ pounds each (*see Note*)
¼ lemon
2 envelopes unflavored gelatin
2 tablespoons sugar

NOTE: *The finished tart should be completely covered with melon balls, one next to the other, forming a solid mass. To be safe, buy a fourth melon to have on hand in case the decoration appears a bit skimpy. Ed.*

HAVE READY:

1. The pastry: Prepare the pastry shell, and bake it completely, following the directions given on pages 214–215.

2. The melons: Choose heavy melons, not excessively ripe, and with a good sweet smell about them.

Cut one of the melons in half, remove the seeds, and, using a melon-ball cutter, form 24 (*or more*) balls. Keep them in the refrigerator to use later for decoration.

Remove the remaining pulp, avoiding any green rind, and pass it through a food mill or sieve into a bowl. Add a squeeze of lemon juice and chill the purée in the refrigerator.

Quarter the remaining two melons, remove the seeds, and scoop out the pulp.

3. Dissolve the gelatin in ¾ cup cold water.

COOKING:

Put the pulp from the two melons, with the sugar, in a heavy casserole. Cook the mixture until most of the water evaporates (*about 30 minutes*) and stir frequently with a wooden spoon.

Then add the softened gelatin, and make sure that it is thoroughly dissolved. Remove the casserole from the stove and, when the mixture has cooled, add the uncooked melon purée.

FINISHING THE TART:

Cover the bottom of the baked pastry shell with the melon mixture and chill it at least 2 hours in the refrigerator. Just before serving, decorate the tart with ice-cold melon balls.

NOTE: *Though this dessert must be well chilled before serving, it must be eaten the same day that it is prepared, or the tart shell will become soggy and the melon balls will become soft. Ed.*

Tarte à la rhubarbe à la crème
RHUBARB TART WITH WHIPPED CREAM

To serve 6:
    1¼ pounds young rhubarb
    ¾ cup sugar, in all
    Zest of 1 lemon, grated
    ½ pound Sweet Pastry Dough (½ recipe *pâte sucrée*, page 32)
    ½ cup *crème fraîche* (page 22), or heavy cream
    Scant ¼ teaspoon ground cloves

PREPARATION OF THE RHUBARB:

Choose the pale young stalks of rhubarb found in the center of the plant. The leaves should be chartreuse and curly; a deep red signifies too much maturity.

Using a small knife, peel back the transparent exterior skin from the rhubarb, as you would strings from a stalk of celery. Cut the rhubarb into pieces approximately 6 inches long, then bunch these together and slice them as thinly as possible.

Put the rhubarb in a heavy casserole with all but 1 tablespoon of the sugar. Cover tightly and stew for 10 minutes over low heat. Remove the cover and raise the heat. Cook, stirring constantly with a wooden spoon, until the excess liquid has evaporated and the rhubarb has the consistency of applesauce. Then add the lemon zest and set the mixture aside.

PREPARATION OF THE PASTRY:

Preheat oven to 425° F.

Roll the dough out into a circle 12 inches in diameter and lay it over a 9- to 10-inch tart form with detachable bottom. Press the dough lightly around the sides of the form and pass the rolling pin across the rim to trim off excess pastry. Prick the bottom of the shell all over with the tines of a fork, then refrigerate the pastry for 15 minutes.

Line the tart shell with a circle of wax paper and weigh down the dough with dried beans or rice. Prebake the pastry for 15 minutes, then remove the beans and wax paper, and fill the shell with the rhubarb sauce. Return the tart to the oven and reduce the heat to 300° F. Bake 20 minutes.

Carefully remove the rim of the tart form and let the dessert cool completely (*allow 2 hours; Ed.*).

FINISHING THE TART:

Just before serving, beat cold *crème fraîche* over ice until it becomes thick and voluminous, but not stiff. Add the remaining sugar and a good pinch of ground cloves, and beat until thoroughly combined.

Using a spatula, spread the whipped cream over the entire surface of the tart and serve immediately.

Le trois-tiers au chocolat
THREE-LAYER CHOCOLATE CAKE
(Color picture 8)

To serve 8:

This cake is a *génoise*, filled with chocolate mousse and whipped cream.

THE MOUSSE:

4½ ounces semisweet baking chocolate
¼ cup milk
2 tablespoons sugar
2 eggs, separated

PREPARE THE MOUSSE A DAY IN ADVANCE:

Melt the chocolate in the milk in the top of a double boiler (*bain-marie*) over very low heat. Add the sugar and egg yolks and, using a wire whisk, stir the mixture off heat and without stopping until it has cooled completely.

Beat the whites until stiff, then, using either a wooden or rubber spatula, carefully incorporate them into the chocolate mixture.

Refrigerate the mousse for at least 12 hours.

THE CAKE:

4 eggs
½ cup sugar
14 tablespoons cornstarch (*see Note*)
4 tablespoons unsweetened cocoa powder, firmly packed (*see Note*)
1½ tablespoons butter for the cake pan

PREPARATION OF THE CAKE:

Prepare the cake early in the day so that it has ample time to become firm before being divided into three layers.

Preheat oven to 325° F.

Place the eggs in a double boiler over hot but not boiling water. Beat them with a wire whisk (*or electric mixer; Ed.*) while slowly adding the sugar, a little at a time. Keep the eggs warm and continue beating until they form a thick ribbon.

NOTE: *It is wise to double-check these measurements:*

14 tablespoons of cornstarch must weigh 4½ ounces and should equal ⅞ cup, loosely packed.

4 tablespoons cocoa powder, firmly packed, should weigh 1 ounce. Ed.

Pass the cornstarch and cocoa powder through a sieve, then add them to the eggs, one after the other, beating until they are completely blended.

NOTE: *The Troisgros specify a cake pan (preferably spring-form) 10 inches in diameter with sides 2½ inches high. When you spread the batter in the pan, it will just reach the sides of the mold; and, after baking, the cake will be scarcely 1 inch in height. Surprisingly, the texture of the cake still lends itself to being divided into three layers. However, a very long, thin knife is crucial to the operation.*

I suggest that you proceed by attempting to divide the cake only into two layers, keeping the knife as close to the top of the cake as possible. After this is accomplished, if cutting either of the two layers in half seems too tricky, then shave off small pieces of cake from the inside of one or both of the layers until you have enough cake to make the third layer. When assembling the cake, use these rough pieces for the middle layer, and no one will be the wiser.

An alternative to this is to give the cake more height by using a smaller cake pan, with a diameter of 8 or 9 inches, and baking it a few minutes longer. Ed.

Grease a 10-inch cake pan liberally with butter and spread the batter within. Bake the cake for 30 minutes. Then remove from the oven, unmold onto a cake rack, and let cool.

INGREDIENTS FOR FINISHING THE CAKE:

1 cup heavy cream
1 tablespoon sugar
3 ounces sliced almonds
1 ounce semisweet baking chocolate

The cream:

Shortly before you are ready to fill and assemble the cake, pour the cream into an ice-cold metal bowl, which has been chilled for some time in the refrigerator or freezer. Beat the cream with a wire whisk (*or electric mixer; Ed.*) for 7 to 8 minutes, or until well thickened. Then add the sugar and mix it in well. Keep the whipped cream cold until you are ready to use it.

ASSEMBLING THE CAKE:

Using a long, slim bread knife, divide the cake horizontally into three equal layers. Place the first layer on a piece of cardboard, cut to the same size as the cake.

Cover this first layer with half of the chocolate mousse, reserving the other half of the mousse.

Put the second layer of cake over the mousse and cover it with whipped cream.

Place the third layer on top, and cover the entire surface with the reserved chocolate mousse. Then refrigerate the cake. *(The layers of filling will be thicker than the layers of cake. Ed.)*

DECORATION:

1. The almonds: Spread the sliced almonds out on a baking sheet, and put them under the broiler; toss them frequently until they are toasted to a light brown. At the last moment before serving, scatter the almonds all over the cake.

2. The chocolate: Finish the cake by shaving the ounce of chocolate with a vegetable peeler, letting the shavings fall as they may over the cake.

NOTE: *An easier way to shave the chocolate is first to soften it on a baking sheet in a 150° F. oven with the door ajar. As soon as the chocolate is malleable, spread it out with a metal spatula, and as it cools, shave it off into curls with a sharp knife. By this method, the chocolate can be prepared in advance. Ed.*

If all the cake is not served immediately, keep it constantly under refrigeration.

La grosse tuile
OVERSIZED ALMOND WAFERS

To make 4 wafers:
   1 heaping cup (5 ounces) slivered blanched almonds
   Butter for the baking sheets
   3 more tablespoons butter, well softened
   ½ cup sugar
   2 egg whites (*from extra-large or jumbo eggs*)
   4 tablespoons cake flour
   ½ teaspoon almond extract

HAVE READY:

1. The almonds: Set aside ⅓ cup of the slivered almonds, and chop the rest.
2. The baking sheets: Choose the number that you think you will need, and butter them liberally, allowing about 1 tablespoon of butter per baking sheet.
3. Preheat oven to 425° F.

NOTE: *Also have ready several rolling pins and/or clean empty bottles so that you will have enough curved surfaces on which to cool the wafers. It should be mentioned that you may encounter some difficulty in lifting wafers of the dimensions given by the Troisgros from the baking sheets and keeping them whole long enough to lay them on the rolling pins or bottles. I suggest that it may be preferable to make wafers of a smaller size that you think manageable, rather than to follow strictly the dimensions given. Ed.*

PREPARATION:

Beat the butter, adding the sugar a little at a time, until the mixture is light and fluffy. Then add the egg whites and continue beating until combined.

Sift the flour over this mixture and, using a rubber spatula, fold in the flour, followed by the shredded almonds and then by the almond extract.

Spread one quarter of the batter out on a prepared baking sheet, forming an oval about 7 inches by 9 inches. It should be very thin, to the point of being transparent; use a fork dipped in ice water to help to accomplish this. If you have a large enough oven, and baking sheet, make more than one wafer at a time.

Sprinkle the unbaked wafers with some of the reserved slivered almonds.

BAKING AND MOLDING THE TILES:

Bake the wafer 5 minutes, or just as long as needed for it to become lightly crisp and golden at the edges. The moment the wafer is done, mold it over a stabilized rolling pin or clean empty bottle, forming in the shape of a *tuile* or roof tile. The wafer should be draped along the length of the rolling pin, not crosswise.

While the first tile cools, proceed with the next one. Unless you have the facilities to prepare several at the same time, repeat this first operation 3 times.

When the tiles have cooled, carefully arrange them on a large attractive platter such as you might use for *petits fours.*

NOTE: *The* tuiles *will stay crisp for several days if kept in an air-tight container. Ed.*

Index

243